Mark Shelton practised in major commercial law firms for thirty years, specialising in property dispute resolution. He has acted for businesses large and small, including FTSE-listed property companies and household-name corporate occupiers, across the whole range of property-related issues. Among other reported cases, he acted for the successful landlord in Shortlands v Cargill [1994], an influential case on the assessment of damages for dilapidations.

He is now a full-time commercial property management law trainer, putting his expertise and experience to good use in training both lawyers and surveyors. He delivers training for providers including MBL Seminars, ForLegal, Professional Conferences, CPT Events, Legal Futures and The Solicitors Group.

A Practical Guide to the Law of Dilapidations

Second Edition

A Practical Guide to the Law of Dilapidations

Second Edition

Mark Shelton

MA (Hons) Law (Cantab), Non-Practising Solicitor

Commercial Property Management Law Trainer

www.marksheltontraining.co.uk

Law Brief Publishing

Published 2022 by Law Brief Publishing, an imprint of Law Brief Publishing Ltd
30 The Parks
Minehead
Somerset
TA24 8BT

www.lawbriefpublishing.com

Paperback: 978-1-914608-82-7

PREFACE TO THE FIRST EDITION

While dilapidations as a practice area has some legal technicality to it, at its heart stands the most practical of issues: a building in need of repair. When it is a building which has been let, the first question is: whose is the responsibility to repair, landlord or tenant? The answer is a short one: look at the lease.

In the residential context, except for long leaseholds, the lease will almost always provide that it is the landlord who is responsible for repair, except perhaps as regards internal decorative order. The focus of this book, though, is on commercial lettings, where repair is generally the tenant's responsibility.

If the building is let to a single tenant, the lease will usually impose on the tenant responsibility for repair of the whole structure.

If it is multi-let, then usually the tenants will be responsible for internal aspects, while the landlord will be responsible for the exterior and structural elements. That said, the cost of repairs carried out by the landlord will ultimately fall on the tenants as well, since it will be recovered through the service charge. It is for this reason that the law relating to what constitutes 'repair' (as opposed to, say, 'improvement'), is to be found partly in the context of tenants' repairing liabilities, and partly in the context of service charge disputes.

Questions of that sort relate to the scope of the obligation, which is a matter of interpreting the lease. The question of who is responsible for repair is, as already indicated, straightforward. The practical issue is more likely to be how to translate that responsibility into the desired outcome.

Perhaps surprisingly, the desired outcome is not always a property in good repair. A landlord may have good reasons for preferring to receive a financial settlement from the tenant, rather than getting his building back in the condition required by the lease. That may depend, of course, on the size of the financial settlement, which requires an assessment of how much the tenant is likely to have to pay in damages for its breaches of repairing obligations. That in turn requires application of legal principles found both in caselaw and in statute.

This is where the legal technicality arises, requiring not only knowledge of the law, but also tactical nous, and awareness of the procedural requirements of the various remedies available to the landlord.

This book provides a practical guide to how the chances of getting the best outcome can be maximised, for both landlord and tenant. The law stated is based on information available up to 18th January 2018.

Mark Shelton
January 2018

PREFACE TO THE
SECOND EDITION

Heraclitus, a Greek philosopher, is often quoted as saying that change is the only constant in life. We may be forgiven for feeling that recent years have rather laboured this point.

The first edition of this book appeared after the Brexit vote, but well before the actual cessation of this country's participation in the institutions of the EU, and two years of uncertainty and political drama still lay ahead. The resolution of the Brexit saga overlapped with the advent of Covid-19, and of course the pandemic still continues, though we may consider ourselves as in recovery. While much of day-to-day life has returned to normality, the global and domestic impacts are still being understood and digested. The recovery from the pandemic itself overlapped with Russia's invasion of Ukraine, bringing a global energy crisis, and triggering levels of inflation not seen for decades in economies across the world. No start or end date can be put on climate change, but it is increasingly a concern which influences policies and decision-making at all levels of human activity.

The relevance of these great matters to this small book is their impact on the occupational terms which landlords and tenants regard as desirable or acceptable. There has been a widespread re-think of standard commercial leasing practices, and dilapidations as a practice area is not immune.

Wider events apart, the law, naturally, does not stand still either, and caselaw emerging since the previous edition merits not only inclusion, but in some instances a reflection on one's previous understanding of the law, and recasting of certain passages. Indeed, the state of one's understanding is also subject to change, and it is therefore hoped that this second edition represents not only an update, but also a refined and expanded version of the original book.

The law stated is based on information available up to 20 September 2022.

Mark Shelton

September 2022

CONTENTS

CHAPTER ONE
UNDERSTANDING THE SCOPE OF THE TENANT'S RESPONSIBILITY TO REPAIR

Content

This chapter examines the extent and nature of the tenant's repairing obligation, including considerations as to interpretation. It also looks beyond the general covenant to repair, to consider other covenants which are relevant to the physical condition of the property.

The repairing obligation is one of the most important elements of a lease, and it will always be expressly provided for, to some extent. In the unlikely event that it is not, the courts are not in the habit of implying repair obligations into leases. Obligations on the landlord as to the repair of specific elements of premises are implied, into shorter residential leases, by *s.11, Landlord and Tenant Act 1985*, though that is outside the scope of this book. Exceptionally, the courts have been prepared to imply an obligation, again on a landlord, where the repair of some element of the building is not provided for at all (see Chapter 2). As regards tenants' repairing obligations, though, it may be taken that in identifying the nature and extent of the obligation, we are concerned only with the content and interpretation of express repairing obligations.

The natural starting-point is the covenant to repair, but other relevant covenants in the lease should not be overlooked.

Covenant to repair

Typical content

In a commercial lease, the tenant will usually be responsible for repair and, in the case of a lease of a whole building, historically the obligation has typically been a 'full' one. The expression 'full repairing obligation' in this sense means an obligation extending to all elements of the building, including major items like the foundations and the roof, whether or not any disrepair pre-dated the grant of the lease.

That said, it is increasingly common for the scope of repairing obligations to be limited. Whereas in the 1980s commercial leases were typically as much as 25 years in duration, the average length of commercial leases being granted now is around five or six years. Twenty-five years is a significant part of the life of a building, and it might be reasonable that a tenant under a 25-year lease should assume responsibility for major structural elements. However, that is very hard to justify in a lease for six years or even less. Increasingly tenants may seek to exclude such elements from their repairing obligation, or limit their repairing obligations by reference to a schedule of condition, so that they are not responsible for any disrepair pre-dating the grant of the lease.

In the case of a letting of part of a building, or part of a development, it is usual for the landlord to have responsibility for the repair of the common parts. It is simply impractical, for example, for each tenant within a shopping centre to be responsible for the repair of one part of the roof. However, it is still the tenants who will pay for any repair work undertaken by the landlord, through the mechanism of the service charge. In such a case, the tenant is likely to have an 'internal repairing obligation' only (the term 'full repairing obligation' is also used by way of contrast to 'internal repairing obligation').

'Internal repairing obligation' is a shorthand expression; the extent of the premises within the tenant's demise, and therefore included within its repairing obligation, will usually be defined. Even in the case of whole-building leases, though, where the repairing obligation will generally be expressed to cover the whole property, attention should still be paid to precisely what is included within the demise. Does it, for example, include subterranean structures and facilities, such as pipes and drains? In certain cases where it is known or anticipated that there may be issues with contaminated land, and the tenant is not prepared to take on any liability for that, the demise may extend only to the surface of the land, and exclude anything beneath; this is known as a 'pie-crust lease'.

A tenant's repairing obligation typically falls into two parts: an obligation to keep the property in repair throughout the term of the lease, and an obligation to leave the property in good repair at the end of the lease. Claims for breach of repairing covenant are mainly brought at the end of the lease (a 'terminal dilapidations claim'), at which time the landlord can rely on both obligations. Until then, it is only the 'throughout the term' obligation which can be relied upon.

Drafting style

In the past, repairing obligations have often been excessively wordy. To take an example from caselaw (*Kitney v Greater London Properties [1984] 2 EGLR 83*):

> *"Well and substantially to repair, renew, uphold, support, maintain, drain, point, pave, cleanse, paint, grain varnish, enamel, distemper, whiten, colour, strip and repaper glaze amend and keep the demised premises ... in good and substantial repair and condition throughout the said term...".*

This style of clause has been judicially stigmatised as "torrential drafting". The courts have had a conflicting approach to the interpretation of such clauses: in some cases taking the view that full meaning should be given to every word of the covenant, and treating them each as imposing a distinct obligation; and in others treating them together as imposing a standard repair obligation. Consistently with the latter view, judges have observed that it does not really matter whether a lease refers to 'good tenantable repair', 'good tenantable repair and condition' 'good and substantial repair and condition', 'thorough repair and good condition', or some similar formula. No particular different standard of repair is intended by those phrases.

It is probably best, when dealing with an older clause of this type, to regard the approach to interpretation as depending on context. The circumstances may suggest that, for example, there was a reason why some part of the premises should be painted specifically with 'distemper' rather than a more usual emulsion 'paint', and if so then 'distemper' should be given that more specific meaning. If, though, there is no reason to suppose that anything more specific than a usual repair obligation was intended, then that is how the clause should be regarded. It is that latter situation which will be more usual.

Reflecting that pragmatism, a modern repairing obligation is likely to say something like:

> *"Throughout the term to put and keep the demised premises in good and substantial repair and condition and to replace and renew where necessary and at the end or sooner determination of the term to yield up the demised premises in good and substantial repair and condition in accordance with the obligations contained in this lease".*

The essence of the obligation is contained in the six words *"good and substantial repair and condition"*, which were used also in the clause quoted above from the *Kitney* case. The modern draftsman, though, is usually satisfied to do without all the other verbiage which was included in that clause.

Even a straightforward modern form of covenant such as that raises issues of interpretation, though.

<u>'put and keep in repair'</u>

Where the tenant is required to 'put and keep' the premises in repair, as is usual, the effect may be to require the tenant to put the premises into a better condition than when it took the lease. Moreover, it was held in *Payne v Haine (1847) 11 JP 462* that a covenant simply to 'keep in repair' must by logical implication include an obligation to put the property in repair, if it is not already; otherwise the tenant cannot perform the obligation to 'keep in repair'. Where a tenant is taking a short lease of a property in poor condition, therefore, they are likely to insist that the full repairing covenant should be qualified by a proviso that they cannot be required to put the premises into any better state of repair than is recorded in a schedule of condition, which is attached to the lease.

No obligation to repair until there is disrepair

Before a repairing obligation can bite, so as to require the tenant to carry out any remedial work, there must be disrepair. In *Post Office v Aquarius Properties [1987] 1 All ER 1055* an office building had been constructed with a defect which allowed water ingress into the basement car park; the car park was regularly inches deep in water, and unusable. While that was undoubtedly inconvenient, until the fabric of the building had deteriorated in some way as a result, there was no disrepair which might oblige the tenant to do anything about the situation.

The court defined disrepair as a "*deterioration from a previous physical condition*". As noted above, the 'previous physical condition' may be judged by reference to a time before the commencement of the lease, if the tenant has either an express or implied obligation to put the property into repair.

The facts of the case are unusual, but it is a useful reminder that the purpose of the repairing covenant is to require the tenant to address disrepair, rather than other problems arising from the physical state of the property.

Obligation to 'keep in good condition'

It is generally considered that a covenant to keep in good condition has a wider meaning than a covenant to repair. This was discussed in *Credit Suisse v Beegas Nominees [1994] 1 EGLR 78*, by way of contrast to *Post Office v Aquarius Properties*. Where there is an obligation to keep the property in a required condition, all that is needed to trigger a requirement to carry out work is that the building should fall short of that condition. That may be the case even if there is no disrepair. Those observations have been quoted with approval since, for example in *Welsh v Greenwich LBC [2000] 3 ELR 41* and *Mason v Totalfinaelf UK Ltd [2003] EWHC 1604 (Ch)*.

The point always seemed to be rather academic, however, in the absence of a reported case in which a 'good condition' obligation was held to impose liability which would not have arisen under a simple 'repair' obligation. That case now exists. *Pullman Foods Ltd v Welsh Ministers [2020] EWHC 2521 (TCC)* concerned a site in Swansea, let to the claimant, Pullman. The Welsh government was the landowner, and served on Pullman a s.25 notice indicating intention to oppose the grant of a new lease. Pullman vacated the site, and subsequently issued proceedings claiming compensation under *s.37* of the *Landlord and Tenant Act 1954*. The Welsh government counterclaimed damages in relation to asbestos-containing materials present at the site upon lease expiry.

The lease contained a tenant's obligation "*at the expiration or sooner determination of the said term quietly and peaceably to deliver up the demised premises leaving the same in good and substantial repair and condition … having first … removed any buildings or works*".

The judge found as a matter of fact that the asbestos had been brought onto site as part of the construction of buildings after and pursuant to the lease. It was held that as the materials had been component parts of the buildings on site, failure to remove them was a breach of the obligation to remove buildings.

As to breach of the 'repair' and 'good condition' obligations, the judge said this:

> "*The covenant in the Lease went beyond one of repair: it was to deliver up the demised premises "in good and substantial repair and condition to the satisfaction of the [Lessor]". In my judgment, use of the word "condition" shows that the obligation was capable of extending to doing works that went beyond repair strictly so called … The mere fact that the demised premises could not be said to be in a state of disrepair would not mean that they were in a good condition.*"

While many leases will deal specifically with liability for land contamination, the case illustrates that general wording as to keeping the premises in good condition may be enough to transfer liability to the tenant.

Obligations to 'maintain' or 'keep in good working order'

Where the clause requires the tenant to 'maintain' the premises, this may only mean not allowing their condition to deteriorate, in which case the word 'maintain' could be regarded as not adding anything to a usual repairing obligation (e.g. *Janet Reger International Ltd v Tiree Ltd [2006] EGLR 131*). This is, though, one of those words whose meaning is likely to depend upon the context; it may carry a sense of ensuring that elements of the property perform their function, as in *Haydon v Kent County Council [1978] QB 343*, where it was held that the duty under the *Highways Act 1959* to maintain the highway included a duty to repair it.

A more straightforward way of expressing an obligation which relates to functionality is a covenant to 'keep in good working order'. This will usually appear in relation to specified elements of the premises such as lifts or air-conditioning, and in that context its meaning is obvious, and requires no further discussion.

Standard of repair

It may also be necessary, in case of dispute, to define to some extent the required standard of repair: if, for example, the doors of the goods lift are scuffed and scratched, will the tenant be expected to leave them as good as new, or is it acceptable to leave them as they are? The expression 'good repair and condition' does not give much assistance in deciding that sort of question. In the absence of any specific and unusual wording, the tenant will be required to put the premises into the state of repair which:

> "*having regard to the age, character, and locality of the house would make it reasonably fit for the occupation of a reasonably-minded tenant of the class who would be likely to take it*" (*Proudfoot v Hart (1890) 25 QBD 42*).

While the wording is slightly quaint to the modern reader, it actually contains useful detail: to identify the required standard, one must look at the age of the building, its character, where it is situated, and who might be in the market for it. The lesson is simply that what standard is appropriate will vary from building to building. The required standard in relation to a modern headquarters office building in the City of London will be very high; however, as regards a 100-year-old corner shop in a tertiary retail location in a depressed regional town, the required standard will be much lower.

So a tenant cannot generally be required to render a 50-year-old property as good as new; but there is a note of caution to be sounded here. The conventional approach to the interpretation of leases (or any other sort of contract for that matter) is to give them the meaning which would have been in the parties' reasonable contemplation at the time the contract was entered into. Therefore, in the case of a ten-year old building let on a lease for a term of 40 years, at the end of the lease the appropriate standard of repair is to be assessed at a time when the building was ten years old, not 50 years old (*Anstruther-Gough-Calthorpe v McOscar [1924] 1 KB 716; Twinmar Holdings Ltd v Klarius UK Ltd [2013] EWHC 944 (TCC)*). Modern lease terms tend to be sufficiently short that this consideration seldom gives rise to difficulties.

The "*age, character and locality*" of the premises may be relevant in deciding whether aesthetic considerations play a part in determining the required standard of repair. In both *Shortlands Investments Ltd v Cargill plc [1995] 1 EGLR 51* and *Sunlife Europe Properties v Tiger Aspect Holdings [2013] EWHC 463*, the court regarded it as unacceptable that only a selection of tiles in a suspended ceiling installation should be cleaned or repaired, as this would leave an unattractive patchwork effect. In the former case, the property concerned was a high-class headquarters office building; in the latter, high-class office and retail premises in a premier area of central London. In each case, when new they had been constructed and fitted out to the highest standard. It seems likely that a court would take a different view in the case of a suspended ceiling in, say, a re-purposed former office premises let to a charity shop.

Improvements

Although, as we have seen, the tenant may be required to 'put' the premises into repair, and therefore to give them back to the landlord in a better condition than that in which they were let, that requirement is limited to matters of repair. The landlord cannot generally require a tenant to carry out improvements to the premises (subject to what is said below about remedying inherent defects). For example, an external wall may require re-rendering; the tenant would be perfectly within its rights to use a relatively inexpensive traditional sand and cement render, if that is what was used originally, even though it would now be possible to use a superior polymer or spraystone render.

That said, the cost of improvements may be recoverable from tenants as part of a dilapidations claim, so long as the improvement is something which is reasonably done by way of remedying disrepair.

Assessing whether works amount to 'improvement' or 'repair' is a question of fact and degree, applying the test in *Ravenseft Properties Ltd v Davstone (Holdings) Ltd [1980] QB 12*, referred to below in relation to inherent defects.

Replacement and renewal

As a matter of ordinary English usage, an obligation to 'repair' has a different meaning from an obligation to 'replace', or 'renew'. Most repairing covenants include specific 'replace and renew' wording, but even where they do not, the courts recognise the reality that repair includes renewal of subsidiary parts (*Lurcott v Wakely [1911] 1 KB 905*). The only way to repair a rotten window-frame, for example, is to replace it.

Where the words 'replace' and 'renew' (or 'rebuild') are expressly included in the repairing covenant, they should not be read as bearing their full literal meaning. They will not, for example, impose on the tenant an obligation to completely replace or renew the property, in the event of total destruction. They must be read in context as part of the repair obligation.

Arguments as to whether works of replacement or renewal go beyond the scope of the repair obligation tend to centre on what is 'subsidiary': in other words, how substantial or significant is the element of replacement. This is a question of fact and degree, and again the *Ravenseft v Davstone* test applies.

Inherent defects

It is a persistent misconception that tenants cannot be required to put right 'inherent defects', that is, faults in the original design. The cases show that inherent defects can fall within a tenant's repairing obligation, so long as it is reasonably necessary to remedy them in order to address disrepair, and so long as they are not too substantial. This is so even though remedying the inherent defect necessarily amounts to an improvement to the premises.

The leading case on this point is *Ravenseft Properties Ltd v Davstone (Holdings) Ltd [1980] QB 12*, which concerned a building constructed with external concrete cladding panels. The cladding had been designed and constructed without expansion joints, with the result that the panels came under stress when they expanded in warm weather, and they had degraded over time. The landlord required the tenant to install new cladding panels, which was clearly work of replacement. The landlord also required the tenant to install expansion joints, which was clearly both an improvement and the remedying of an inherent defect.

However, the degradation of the panels was clearly disrepair, and therefore the repairing obligations were engaged. The cladding panels were subsidiary parts, and their replacement was required to effect the necessary repairs. As to the expansion joints, the problem would simply recur if the cladding were to be replaced without any, which made it reasonably necessary to install expansion joints in order to address the disrepair, and brought this element of the work within the scope of the tenant's repairing obligation.

Neither was the work sufficiently substantial or significant to go beyond the scope of 'repair'. Having considered the authorities in relation to the distinctions between 'repair' and 'improvement', and between 'repair' and 'replacement' or 'renewal', the court held that the test to be applied was whether or not requiring the tenant to do the work would mean the landlord getting back at lease expiry a building which was wholly different from that which had been let. This test is not particularly easy to apply, but it can at least be said that there comes a point at which work which amounts to improvement or replacement, or work carried out to put right an inherent defect, which because is it carried out in the context of remedying disrepair is in principle the tenant's responsibility, will nevertheless be considered too substantial or significant to fall within the tenant's repairing covenant.

In *City of London v Leaseholders of Great Arthur House [2021] EWCA Civ 431*, a distinction was drawn between 'inherent defects' and 'structural defects'. The case was concerned with whether the landlord was entitled to recover the costs of certain repair works via the service charge, and the lease provided that the landlord was not entitled to recover the costs of remedying 'structural defects'. The court considered that the expression was not confined to 'inherent defects', but included defects in workmanship as well as design, so long as they affected the structure of the building. If there had been no deterioration since the defect existed, then it was not caught by the repairing obligation (*Post Office v Aquarius Properties [1987] 1 All ER 1055*, above). If the need for repair was a result of damage or deterioration over time then the work would be 'repair' whether or not it related to a structural element of the building; nevertheless if the effect would be (a) to remedy a structural defect, then the fact that it would *also* (b) put right deterioration over time, did not cancel out (a). The landlord would not be entitled to recover the cost of that work.

The case was concerned with a specific piece of drafting, and its general application is perhaps limited.

Covenant to decorate

Leases will commonly impose an obligation to decorate, externally or internally or both, usually at regular intervals throughout the term (often every five years), and in the last year of the term. There is a significant overlap here with the general repairing covenant, since 'good repair' may include 'good decorative order' to a large extent. Nevertheless, different considerations as to the assessment of damages for breach may apply in some instances.

Covenant to reinstate alterations

Where the tenant has carried out any alterations to the property, there is usually a requirement to reinstate the alterations at the end of the term. Nowadays this is often at the landlord's option, rather than an automatic obligation. Care needs to be taken in reviewing the lease documentation when dealing with dilapidations and reinstatement at the end of the term, since the obligations as they appear in the lease may have been varied to some extent by the provisions of any licence to alter. Again, the assessment of damages for breach of a covenant to reinstate differs from that for breach of a repairing covenant.

Covenant to comply with statute

Leases generally shift onto the tenant the burden of compliance with any statutory requirement concerning the premises. This may mean that, for example, fire precautions works, disability adjustment works, even remediation of contaminated land, will be the tenant's responsibility, regardless of whether there is any disrepair.

Obligation not to commit waste

The law relating to waste is archaic, and is rarely of practical significance. 'Voluntary waste' means damaging the premises by some deliberate or negligent act, and this is more to do with alterations. Liability for voluntary waste arises in tort independently of what the lease may say, but it is often addressed in the tenant's lease covenants as well. 'Permissive waste' means damaging the premises by failure to act, and obviously covers much the same sort of territory as express covenants to repair.

Permissive waste was examined thoroughly in *Dayani v Bromley LBC (No. 1) [1999] 3 EGLR 144*, where it was considered that the obligation is limited to maintaining the premises in the condition in which they were at lease commencement. It is in effect much like a repairing obligation limited by a schedule of condition. The court also held that tenants under fixed-term leases, unlike periodic tenants or tenants at will, are liable for permissive waste by virtue of *s.2, Statute of Marlborough 1267*, whether or not there is an express covenant to that effect in the lease.

It is common, at any rate, to see an express covenant not to commit waste, whether voluntary or permissive, and there may be occasions when something falls outside the scope of the express repairing obligation, but arguably within the scope of the obligation not to commit waste, so the covenant is potentially a useful fall-back protection for the landlord.

Costs of preparing the schedule

The starting-point in procedural terms for enforcing repairing liability against a tenant is the preparation of a schedule of dilapidations by the landlord's building surveyor. This obviously requires a site visit by the building surveyor, and depending on the nature of the property and the extent of the disrepair, this may take a number of days. The schedule will then be prepared, often in a spreadsheet or other electronic format, listing the various items of disrepair individually, and often by reference to professionally-taken photographs. The costs involved in having a schedule of dilapidations prepared can run into thousands of pounds, and landlords will want to recover those costs from their tenants.

Whether those costs are recoverable as part of the damages for breach of the tenant's repairing covenants is the subject of conflicting authority. In *Maud v Sandars [1943] 2 All ER 783* it was held that the costs were not recoverable as damages. They were not caused by the tenant's breach of covenant, but were incurred by the landlord in order to investigate the amount he was able to claim from the tenant. However, in *PGF II SA v Royal & Sun Alliance Insurance Plc [2011] 1 P&CR 11*, the landlord was able to recover £6,000 plus VAT in respect of the schedule costs, on the basis that *"The schedule is required as a direct consequence of the tenant's breach of covenant"*. It appears therefore that in any individual case it will be necessary to analyse whether and to what extent the costs were caused by the breach of covenant, unless there is a separate express covenant which covers the matter.

Most leases contain a provision to the effect that the landlord is entitled to recover from the tenant the costs of preparing and serving a notice under *s.146* of the *Law of Property Act 1925* (the preliminary to forfeiture of the lease). Where the s.146 notice is served together with a schedule of dilapidations, the schedule costs would usually be recoverable under such a provision (*Johnsey Estates v Secretary of State for the Environment (6 August 1999) (unreported)*). Landlords may try to take advantage of this, where there is such a provision in the lease, by attaching a s.146 notice to the schedule, even though they do not intend to forfeit the lease, and indeed even though the notice and schedule are served so late in the day that the lease will expire before any forfeiture could be effected. These considerations prevented recovery of schedule costs in the *Johnsey Estates* case, and also in *Lintott Property Developments v Bower [2005] All E R (D) 454*. To recover schedule costs in this way, the s.146 notice must genuinely have been intended as a precursor to forfeiture.

However, it is increasingly common to find a wider provision, entitling the landlord to recovery of professional fees and costs under various heads, typically including the costs of preparation and service of a schedule of dilapidations. *Riverside Property Investments v Blackhawk Automotive [2005] 1 EGLR 114* provides one instance of a landlord recovering schedule costs under such a provision. Whether a particular clause extends to schedule costs, and if so what amount is recoverable, must of course be a question of construction. It is often the case that a clause of this sort leaves it unclear whether the costs must be incurred and demanded prior to lease expiry in order to be recoverable.

Summary

While modern repairing covenants are typically quite short and standard in their wording, there are several features of their drafting and interpretation which have practical importance:

- Care is required in identifying the extent of the premises which are the subject of the repairing obligation.

- If the premises were in disrepair at the date of the lease, the obligation is likely to extend to bringing the premises into good repair.

- The obligation may however be limited by reference to a schedule of condition.

- The required standard of repair is assessed by reference to the age, character and location of the particular property, and who is likely to be in the market for it.

- The tenant may be responsible for improvements, replacement of subsidiary elements of the property, and even putting right defects inherent in the original design and construction of the property, so long as the work forms part of an appropriate method of addressing disrepair.

- However, the tenant cannot be responsible for work the effect of which is to give back to the landlord at lease expiry a wholly different property from that which was let. This is a question of fact and degree.

- Also, unless there has been some deterioration in the physical condition of the property, the repair obligation is not triggered.

The repairing obligation is not the only one which relates to the physical condition of the property, and consideration must also be given to covenants to decorate, covenants to reinstate alterations, covenants to comply with statute, the obligation not to commit waste, and covenants to bear the cost of preparation of a schedule of dilapidations.

It may be important also to consider whether the scope of any relevant obligations have been varied in ancillary documents such as licences to alter.

CHAPTER TWO
ANTICIPATING ISSUES BEFORE LEASE COMMENCEMENT

Content

This chapter addresses the potential for prevention of claims, by a sharper focus on repair obligations before a lease comes into being.

Before going on to consider the actions that may be taken by a landlord to enforce repairing and related obligations, it is worth considering how what is done or not done prior to the grant of the lease can lead to difficulties later on, for both landlord and tenant.

Experience suggests that many small businesses manage without professional advice of any sort when taking a lease, and this is often storing up problems for the future. Even when solicitor and surveyor are retained, pressure on fee arrangements may mean that their input is relatively limited.

Due diligence

As regards matters concerning the physical condition of a property, the familiar rule is '*caveat emptor*' – let the buyer beware. That applies to tenants taking business leases just as much as it does to someone buying a house. It is therefore for the tenant to investigate the state of the property, and consider what that means in relation to taking on repairing liability. Investigations usually comprise two elements: a survey, and pre-lease enquiries.

Despite both those exercises having been undertaken, problems may sometimes be discovered even shortly after completion, when the tenant may find, for example, that fit-out works reveal the presence of asbestos at the property; or perhaps that the air-conditioning is erratic in operation, or the electricity supply needs to be upgraded for their requirements. In the longer term, when a dilapidations claim comes to be brought, the tenant may discover that even issues of which they were aware turn out to be more extensive in their effect, and more expensive to remedy, than had been anticipated.

Fee constraints on the surveyor may be one factor in this, but another can be that the urgency of completing the transaction overrides other considerations. A retail tenant, for example, may be desperate to complete the lease in time to benefit from the pre-Christmas trading period.

Certain specialist surveyors offer 'technical due diligence' services, and will thoroughly interrogate all physical aspects of the building by reference to the incoming tenant's operational requirements and the impact of the repairing obligations they will be undertaking. That sort of investigation may be prohibitively expensive except for major lettings.

As regards responses to pre-lease enquiries, there is no obligation on landlords to respond at all, although if they do they are required to be full and frank in their replies. There may be an obligation to update the tenant, if and when the position as set out in their replies changes, running up to completion. Leases may contain 'entire agreement' clauses, which protect the landlord from liability for any replies, apart from those given in writing; this means, of course, that tenants must insist on written replies.

It may be that a landlord will respond along the lines of 'tenant must make their own enquiries' or 'we are not aware, tenant must rely upon their own inspection'. Replies of this sort are often accepted uncritically as simply the normal course of a routine conveyancing transaction, but matters relating to the physical condition of a property should be within the landlord's knowledge, and it may be worth trying to insist upon a substantive reply.

Particularly when a building is old, it can be a useful exercise for tenant, surveyor and solicitor to sit around a table together (and indeed inspect the building together) to understand the tenant's operational requirements, and the extent of the repairing obligations which the landlord is proposing, against the actual configuration and condition of the building.

There is of course a cost to that sort of exercise, but set against the potential costs of repair at lease expiry, it can be money well-spent. In *Sunlife Europe Properties v Tiger Aspect Holdings [2013] EWHC 463 (TCC)* the tenant had taken an assignment of the lease in 2000. The building was around 30 years old at that time, and there was significant disrepair. The tenant therefore negotiated to receive a reverse premium of £490,000 on taking the assignment, to cover the accrued dilapidations liability. Thirteen years later, following lease expiry, the outcome of the case was an actual dilapidations liability in excess of £1m. One can only speculate as to whether additional due diligence would have led to negotiation of a significantly larger premium, but the case illustrates the potential impact of end-of-term liabilities, which may be many times more than the likely fees involved in pre-lease investigations.

Scope of repair obligations

Dilapidations disputes can arise out of features of the lease drafting which prove to be less than ideal; again, this can be ultimately due to time pressures or to fee constraints, so that not enough time is spent on the matter, or it is delegated to junior staff. This can be as much of a headache for landlords as it is for tenants. Common and obvious issues include inconsistences, split or ill-defined obligations, and gaps in the scheme of obligation.

Inconsistencies

Problems of inconsistency typically arise in relation to documents supplemental and subsequent to the lease, such as deeds of variation, or licences to alter. For example, the lease may exempt alterations from the scope of the repair covenants, but provide for reinstatement at the end of the term, while the licence may provide that all the tenant's covenants in the lease, including repair, apply to the alterations, while providing for reinstatement only if required by the landlord.

Even within the lease, though, internal inconsistencies can be encountered. An example from caselaw is *Holding & Barnes Plc v Hill House Hammond [2002] 2 P&CR 11*. The lease in that case was one of seven entered into on the same day between the same parties, as part of the sale of an insurance business. Five of them related to parts of buildings, while two (including the one which was the subject of this dispute) related to whole buildings. The repair obligation had obviously been copied over from one of the leases of part, and provided that the landlord was to "*keep the structure of the Building (other than those parts comprised in the property) in good and tenantable repair and condition*". Since this was a lease of the whole, there was no distinction between 'the Building' and 'the property', and the clause was a nonsense. (In the event, the court concluded that the words in brackets were to be ignored).

Split or ill-defined obligations

It has been mentioned previously that, in the case of a letting of part, the extent of the internal demise will usually be defined. This is done with varying degrees of exactitude.

A reasonably detailed definition might, for example, specify that the demise includes such matters as:

- plaster, paint and any other internal surfacing materials on structural walls forming part of the boundary of the premises;

- windows and window-frames, excluding external decorative finishes of external windows;

- one half severed vertically of non-structural walls separating the premises from other units;

- raised floors; and

- suspended ceilings.

That degree of detail is really useful when it comes to determining responsibility for repair.

Short, relatively informal leases prepared at low cost, perhaps on standard forms, may go into much less detail, and might, for example, simply make the tenant responsible for 'the interior' of the premises, while the landlord undertakes responsibility for 'the exterior'. If the window-frames are rotten, it is then impossible to identify whose is the responsibility, and a negotiated contribution from the tenant is the most likely outcome.

Gaps in the scheme of obligation

Issues sometimes arise in multi-let properties, where the landlord has not taken on a repairing obligation as regards the common parts. Since it is landlords who prepare leases, a landlord might give itself the right to recover, via the service charge, the cost of, say, fixing the roof, but reserve to itself absolute discretion over whether it does fix the roof, by simply omitting to include in the lease any obligation to do so. What then happens where the top-floor tenant is in breach of its internal repairing obligation because water ingress is damaging the internal finishes, but the water ingress is caused by the leaky roof?

There have been attempts in such situations to imply a so-called correlative repairing obligation on the landlord, for example in *Barrett v Lounova (1982) Ltd [1990] 1 QB 348*. That case concerned a house, let on a monthly periodic residential tenancy. The problem was water ingress, caused by disrepair to the outside of the property. The tenancy agreement contained an express covenant by the tenant to keep the inside of the property in repair, but was silent as to any obligation on either party to repair the outside. The tenant's covenant was enforceable throughout the tenancy, and could not be properly performed unless the outside was kept in repair.

In the circumstances, an obligation by the landlord to repair the outside, correlative to the tenant's obligation to repair the inside, was implied in order to give business efficacy to the agreement.

This is rarely successful, though. *Janet Reger International Ltd v Tiree Ltd [1996] EWHC 1743 (Ch)* is one example. The case concerned basement and ground floor retail premises in Beauchamp Place, Knightsbridge. There was extensive damp penetration and damage over a long period of time, ultimately found to require installation of a new damp-proof course in the basement, extending to 1m above ground level. The landlord denied responsibility, and the work was ultimately found not to fall within the landlord's covenant "*to use reasonable endeavours to maintain, repair and renew the Structure*", because the existing damp-proof course, though defective, was not in disrepair. It had always been defective, and there had been no deterioration in its condition.

That left the tenant to try to persuade the court that a term should be implied into the lease that "*the Landlord will remedy any defective part of the Structure which causes damage to part of the Demised Premises*". The court considered that no such term was required to give business efficacy to the agreement, and therefore one should not be implied.

Implication of contract terms

On what basis, then can terms be implied into a lease (or any other contract)? The issue of implication of terms arises where the express wording of a contract, properly construed, fails to address at all the point at issue in the case. The question is, in that event, whether there is any scope for saying that a term should be implied into the contract in order to spell out the parties' true intentions.

In the traditional approach, the court applies two tests: the 'officious bystander' test, and the 'business efficacy' test. In the modern law, though, the process of implication is regarded as simply another aspect of construction of the contract. In the leading case of *Attorney General of Belize v Belize Telecom [2009] 1 WLR 1988* Lord Hoffmann said:

"The court has no power to improve upon the instrument which it is called upon to construe, whether it be a contract, a statute or articles of association. It cannot introduce terms to make it fairer or more reasonable. It is concerned only to discover what the instrument means".

Thus the traditional tests for implying a term are not separate bases, but simply expressions of one central principle:

"... in every case in which it is said that some provision ought to be implied in an instrument, the question for the court is whether such a provision would spell out in express words what the instrument, read against the relevant background, would reasonably be understood to mean. ... this question can be reformulated in various ways which a court may find helpful in providing an answer – the implied term must 'go without saying', it must be 'necessary to give business efficacy to the contract' and so on – but these are not ... to be treated as different or additional tests. There is only one question: is that what the instrument, read as a whole against the relevant background, would reasonably be understood to mean?"

The threshold for implying a term is high. The default position is that if the contract makes no provision for a given event, nothing is to happen. The more detailed and carefully drafted the agreement the harder it will be to dislodge this usual inference.

As the court said in *Janet Reger*:

"... the courts are reluctant to imply a term where, as here, there is a long and complex legal document drawn up by the lawyers in which the parties have crystallised the terms of their relationship".

In *Stonecrest Marble Ltd v Shepherds Bush Housing Association Ltd [2021] EWHC 2621 (Ch)*, the court noted:

"... the Lease is a detailed document, which runs to 48 pages and which was professionally drafted. The parties to the Lease were commercially sophisticated. Therefore, significant weight must be

attached to the language that the parties have chosen to express their agreement."

The implication must be necessary to give business efficacy to the contract. This does not mean that it must be necessary to make the contract work at all, but that it must be *"essential to give effect to the reasonable expectations of the parties"* (*Equitable Life v Hyman [2002] 1 AC 408*).

The implication must also be objectively obvious from the viewpoint of both parties. It need not be immediately obvious; it may require careful consideration of the contract as a whole in its commercial and factual context. In the light of that consideration, the implication will only be made if it is clear that it gives effect to what the contract *"must mean"* (*Crema v Cenkos Securities [2011] 1 WLR 2066*).

The implied term must also be reasonable, capable of clear expression and must not contradict the express provisions of the contract.

Nature of implied obligation

Where an implied obligation is found to exist, it may be of a limited nature. In *Cockburn v Smith [1924] 2 KB 119* the landlords owned a block of flats and were found liable to the top floor tenant for damage suffered by her as a result of water ingress caused by a defect in the guttering. The landlords had notice of the defects. One of the members of the court considered that:

> *"... the question is what duty the landlords owed to the plaintiff in relation to this defective guttering. It cannot now be suggested that there was any agreement, express or implied, which can accurately be described as an agreement to repair the roof or guttering; but there is a line of authorities to show that a landlord is under an obligation to take reasonable care that the premises retained in his occupation are not in such a condition as to cause damage to the parts demised to others."*

In *Duke of Westminster v Guild [1985] QB 688*, the tenant claimed damages in respect of loss suffered by him through the landlord's failure to repair a drain which in part ran below the property retained by the landlord. It was held that there were no special factors requiring the lease to be interpreted to give it business efficacy by imposing on the landlords an obligation to carry out repairs. No obligation on the landlord was to be implied.

However, having considered the relevant authorities, including *Cockburn v Smith*, it was further held that there is a general principle that:

> *"Where the lessor retains in his possession and control something ancillary to the premises demised, such as a roof or staircase, the maintenance of which in proper repair is necessary for the protection of the demised premises or the safe enjoyment of them by the tenant, the lessor is under an obligation to take reasonable care that the premises retained in his occupation are not in such a condition as to cause damage to the tenant or to the premises demised."*

It is generally considered that the nature of this obligation is such that it only arises where the defect in the retained parts results in damage to the tenant or the demised premises. Any implied obligation is therefore likely to fall short of an actual repairing obligation, and will be limited to disrepair of which the landlord has notice, and which has caused damage.

<u>Stonecrest Marble – bringing the principles together</u>

A good recent example of the application of these principles is supplied by *Stonecrest Marble Ltd v Shepherds Bush Housing Association Ltd [2021] EWHC 2621 (Ch)*, which also illustrates another problem in the way of implied terms, namely the existence of a 'scheme of repair'.

Stonecrest held a commercial lease of a unit in a property that consisted of commercial premises at ground floor level, and residential premises above. Shepherds Bush Housing Association was its landlord. Following the grant of the lease, Stonecrest traded from the unit, selling tiles. In August 2017, and during a period when Stonecrest had stopped trading at the unit, it reported water ingress into the unit, which appeared to come from the retained parts and at times of heavy rainfall. After a period of two years, experts for the parties agreed that the cause of the water ingress was the gradual accumulation of debris in a drainage gutter in the retained parts, from which the water overflowed and entered the commercial unit.

The lease included a tenant covenant to keep the unit in good repair and condition. However, the landlord's covenants were more limited. They included:

- a covenant to use reasonable endeavours to repair, maintain, clean and light the roads, paths and parking areas in the common parts

- a statement that "*the landlord may, but shall not be obliged to, provide any of the other Services* [being a list of items for which the landlord could demand a service charge]", and

- a statement that "*the landlord shall not be obliged to carry out any repair where the need for that repair has arisen by reason of any damage or destruction by a risk against which the landlord is not obliged to insure*".

There was then a landlord's insurance covenant in common form, and the insured risks included "*... overflowing of water ... apparatus*". However, the obligation to insure was expressed to be subject to "*any exclusions, limitations, excesses and conditions that may be imposed by the insurers*". As might be expected, the landlord's insurance policy clearly excluded cover where the damage was caused by, or consisted of, gradual deterioration or wear and tear.

Following the water ingress, Stonecrest contended that the landlord was in breach of the covenant for quiet enjoyment, or alternatively a duty imposed at common law, for having failed to investigate the cause of the water ingress and carry out the necessary work to unblock the gutter. It claimed damages for loss of profits and damage to the unit.

This looks very similar at first sight to the circumstances of *Cockburn v Smith*, where the court found that there was an implied obligation on the landlord, although of a limited nature, as discussed previously. The legal basis for such an obligation had been considered in *Gavin v Community Housing Association Limited [2013] EWCA Civ*, where it was held that the obligation to take reasonable care arises in contract as an implied term, rather than in tort.

Given that in this case, the tenant had pleaded its case on the basis of breach of the covenant for quiet enjoyment, or alternatively breach of a duty imposed at common law, it followed that the tenant's claim failed, since it had not alleged any implied term.

The court went on to consider the terms of the lease, on the basis that whether an obligation might otherwise arise as an implied term, or in tort, it could be excluded by the express terms of the lease:

> *"... the precise ... basis of liability may not matter in cases where ... the parties have a contractual relationship under the terms of the lease. Whether the duty imposed on the landlord to take reasonable care of the retained premises arises in tort or contract, the court has still to consider whether the express scheme of repair or insurance imposed by the lease excludes any other form of liability which the law might otherwise impose."*

The court also relied upon *Gavin v Community Housing Association* to hold that the express terms of the lease established a 'comprehensive scheme of repair and insurance', which ruled out the implication of any additional term. To imply a term:

> *"... would be to seek to improve the contract from the point of view of the tenant rather than to give it the meaning and effect which both parties must have intended given the terms and structure of their contract."*

As to identifying the existence of a scheme of repair the judge said, referring to the lease:

"So far as the quality of the drafting, it does not lack clarity and it is neither illogical nor incoherent. The Lease in clear and unambiguous terms provides that

> *(i)   T is responsible for keeping the Property in good repair and condition*
>
> *(ii) L expressly has no obligation to repair in circumstances where L has no obligation to insure*
>
> *(iii) L is obliged to insure the Property against loss or damage caused by a relatively long list of named risks, but subject to any exclusions, limitations, excesses and conditions that may be imposed by the insurers, and*
>
> *(iv) L is obliged to use the insurance monies received to repair the Property.*

In my judgment … [t]he parties intended that the Lease provide a comprehensive scheme for the repair of both the Property and the Retained Parts"

It did not matter, as the tenant sought to argue, that there might be some gaps in the scheme, with the result that the tenant might suffer loss. Incomplete protection does not of and by itself mean that the parties did not intend the lease to provide a comprehensive scheme of repair and insurance.

There was therefore no express or implied obligation under the lease for the landlord to repair or keep in repair the retained parts. The tenant could not, in those circumstances, rely upon the covenant for quiet enjoyment as an alternative means of imposing a positive obligation on the landlord which they would not otherwise be obliged to perform.

The case is an important reminder to scrutinise the terms of the lease carefully. If the court concludes that the parties have created a scheme of repair and insurance under the lease, which excludes any landlord liability, then there is no basis for bringing a claim against a landlord in such circumstances.

'Whole agreement' clauses

So-called 'whole agreement' clauses can also be a hurdle to overcome, though because an implied term is considered always to have been part of the agreement, a clause of this type does not rule out the implication of a term.

Hipwell v Szurek [2018] EWCA Civ 674, is an instance of a tenant successfully getting around a 'whole agreement' clause by establishing an implied repair obligation. The tenant had closed down her business after experiencing problems as a result of unsafe electrical wiring. She alleged that her landlord had falsely or negligently represented to her that the premises had been rewired and had passed an inspection. She claimed she was entitled to rescind the lease. She also claimed that her lease contained an implied term whose effect was that the landlord was responsible for maintaining and repairing electrical installations.

The lease did not contain any express obligations in relation to either the exterior of the premises or the plumbing and electrical installation and supply. The lease did have a clause stating that it constituted the "*entire agreement and understanding of the parties relating to the transaction*". It also had a clause in which the tenant acknowledged that in entering into the lease she "*was not relying on, and would have no remedy in respect of, any statement or representation made by the landlord*".

The Court of Appeal held that there was a plain and obvious gap in the lease in relation to responsibility for the exterior of the premises and its plumbing/electrical installation and supply. That gap was inconsistent with the parties' objective intentions. To ensure that the lease did not lack commercial or practical coherence, the gap had to be plugged by implying a covenant on the landlord's part to the effect that the electrical installation and other service media provided was safely installed and continued to be covered by any requisite certificate.

Unlike the lease in *Stonecrest Marble*, the lease in this case was poorly drafted, so that no comprehensive scheme of repair and insurance was identifiable, and the court could take the view that the intentions of the parties needed to be spelled out in the implied term. Although the result was ultimately success for the tenant, a trip to the Court of Appeal is an expensive and slow way of achieving it. Clarity and comprehensive drafting, as always, saves litigation in the end.

Implied terms – summary

Where does all this caselaw leave us?

- A term will only be implied if the court considers it necessary to give effect to the common intentions of the parties.

- Finding out what the common intentions were requires consideration of the express terms of the lease. There should be enough relevant content to identify the parties' intentions, but not too much: the more comprehensive, detailed and carefully drafted the lease is, the less likely it is that the court will consider a term should be implied. A comprehensive scheme of repair and insurance will oust any further obligation upon the landlord.

- In the case of a multi-let property where the landlord retains parts of the building, there can be an implied obligation to take reasonable care that the retained parts are not in such a condition as to cause damage to the tenant or to the demised premises, though this too can be ousted by a comprehensive scheme of repair and insurance.

- In the absence of any express or implied term, the tenant cannot rely upon the quiet enjoyment covenant to impose any positive obligation upon the landlord.

The cases in which liability has been imposed upon the landlord usually feature poor lease drafting, and it will usually be an uphill struggle to establish an implied obligation where that is not the case.

Schedules of condition

The role of schedules of condition has been mentioned previously; they identify the state of repair of the property at the time the lease is granted, and limit the tenant's repair obligation, so that it is not obliged to leave the property in any better state than that.

From the tenant's point of view, therefore, the usefulness of the schedule of condition will arise at the end of the lease. The landlord has a different focus: without conceding a schedule of condition, the landlord would itself have to spend money on repairing the property, before being able to let with a full repairing obligation. The function of the schedule from the landlord's point of view is to facilitate a letting, and its usefulness to him is exhausted as soon as the property is let.

That difference of approach can matter, because of its implications as regards the preparation of the schedule. It would be rare, though ideal, for the schedule to be prepared by an independent third party, at the joint cost of the landlord and tenant. It is more likely to be prepared by the landlord's surveyor, and there will be no incentive to spend significant time preparing anything which will have real evidential value in the event of a dispute at lease expiry. It can sometimes be the case that the preparation of the schedule of condition is left to the tenant, and typically they will have little idea of what is required.

What one would ideally wish to see, defending a dilapidations claim for a tenant with the benefit of a schedule of condition, is something that looks very like a schedule of dilapidations: a detailed, item-by-item description of the disrepair, cross-referenced to good-quality photographs. All too often, there is no description at all; what has happened in fact is that someone has taken a series of photographs, possibly using their phone. The photographs will have been downloaded and printed, perhaps in black and white to save money. They may then have been photocopied repeatedly. The end of the process is that bound into the back of the lease is several pages of grainy photocopies of photographs, which make it very difficult to establish what the state of the property was.

Even a well-prepared schedule may have restricted usefulness, however. If a schedule records, say, 50 broken or missing roof tiles, and at lease expiry there are 125, then the tenant's obligation is to repair the additional 75. Bearing in mind the labour cost and hire of scaffolding, this may make little difference. Or perhaps the schedule records that a flat roof is heavily patched; at lease expiry it is found to be in need of complete replacement. The tenant is not responsible for the complete replacement; however it is responsible for the additional deterioration. Its obligation is to give back to the landlord a building with a partially deteriorated roof, which is clearly absurd. All the schedule does in that situation is to provide a not-very-satisfactory basis for negotiating a contribution to the cost of replacement.

None of this means that tenants should not bother with schedules of condition. It is better to have one than not. But a schedule of condition is not a 'magic bullet', and tenants can perhaps think creatively about other ways of limiting the repair obligation, such as a financial cap, or an obligation to spend a certain sum per year on repair, or excluding identified elements of the building from the obligation to repair.

Informal occupation

Uncertainty over the existence or scope of repairing obligations can be an issue for landlords in cases of informal occupation. In a weak letting market, the overriding priority of just having someone in the property paying rent can often deflect focus away from getting obligations documented properly.

These factual situations are all familiar examples:

- The tenant is desperate to take occupation, but the legal paperwork is not yet finalised. They are allowed into occupation, and it then proves impossible to get them to sign up.

- A contracted-out lease has expired, however rent has continued to be demanded and accepted.

- A tenant goes into an insolvency procedure. The landlord discovers that there is another "phoenix" occupier. They continue to pay the rent and the landlord tolerates the situation for the time being.

When the landlord comes to make a dilapidations claim in this sort of situation, the problem will be establishing the legal basis for the occupation, and more particularly any terms in relation to the repair of the property. Often there are no express repair obligations, and a landlord may have to attempt to rely upon the law of permissive waste, which is very much less certain.

Summary

A lack of attention to the physical state of the property, and its implications as regards repair liabilities at the end of the term, is often a source of difficulties, particularly for small business tenants who do not retain professional advisers upon taking a lease.

There are a number of steps that can be taken to limit the likelihood of problems later on:

- Instructing specialist surveyors to conduct a 'technical due diligence' exercise.

- Insisting on substantive replies to pre-lease enquiries, where the subject-matter should be within the landlord's actual knowledge.

- Considering the state of repair, the configuration of the building and services, the proposed repairing obligation and the tenant's operational requirements, at a round-table meeting between tenant, surveyor and solicitor.

- As part of such a round-table exercise or otherwise, focusing on lease drafting issues in relation to repair, with a view to avoiding inconsistencies, split or ill-defined obligations, and gaps in the scheme of obligation.

- Insisting on a detailed and well-prepared schedule of condition, and/or considering other possible limitations on the repair obligation.

- Avoiding and/or regularising informal occupation.

CHAPTER THREE

MID-TERM DILAPIDATIONS (1) – DAMAGES, SPECIFIC PERFORMANCE AND DECLARATORY RELIEF

Content

This chapter outlines the effect of the Leasehold Property (Repairs) Act 1938, and two of the potential remedies for addressing breach of repairing obligation during the term of a lease: damages, specific performance and declaratory relief.

In principle, the usual contractual remedies of damages and specific performance are available in relation to breach of a repairing obligation, just as they are for breach of any other contractual term. In the context of leases, landlords usually have the further remedy of forfeiture of the lease, in the event of any breach of covenant by the tenant (this will be considered in the next chapter). In practice, however, a combination of statute and caselaw restrict the availability of these remedies to a considerable extent, at least during the lease term. The remedy which is perhaps most likely to be used mid-term is the procedure endorsed by the Court of Appeal in *Jervis v Harris [1996] Ch 195*, often referred to as a 'repair notice', or the 'self-help' procedure, or a 'Jervis v Harris claim' (this will also be considered in the following chapter).

At lease expiry all of these remedies, with the exception of a claim for damages, cease to be relevant or available. At the same time, some of the problems with damages claims simply fall away after the end of the lease term. This is why landlords generally tend to put off dealing with dilapidations until then (particularly given that lease terms are now often only a few years in duration). It is much more common to see a 'terminal dilapidations claim' than a 'mid-term dilapidations claim'. However, there may sometimes be reasons which make it very important for landlords to be able to address the issue of disrepair in mid-term.

- This may be because the disrepair existing at a particular property is very serious, the lease has many years to run, and there is good reason to think the tenant will do nothing about the disrepair unless forced to do so.

- Also, leaving disrepair until lease-end, in the expectation of receiving a financial settlement, runs a risk of the tenant not having the means to pay at that time.

- Another reason to deal with dilapidations before lease-end is the potential problem upon lease renewal. Rent for the renewal lease is determined under *s.34* of the *Landlord and Tenant Act 1954*. The 1954 Act pre-dated the wide prevalence of rent review as a feature of commercial leases, so valuation under *s.34* diverges from usual rent review practice in a few respects. While it would be standard that a rent review clause should direct the valuer to disregard any breach of tenant's repairing covenant, or to assume that the premises are in good repair, there is no such provision in *s.34*. The result is that the tenant can potentially profit by its own default: by breaching the repair obligation, it reduces the rental value of the property, and so benefits from a lower rent upon renewal. There are dicta in certain cases suggesting that the court should follow rent review practice in relation to this issue (e.g. *Family Management v Gray [1980] 1 EGLR 46* and *Lyndendown v Vitamol [2007] 3 EGLR 11*), though there is no case in which a court has actually determined the rent for a renewal lease on the basis of having resolved the issue in that way. A landlord may therefore wish to have disrepair dealt with before renewal, to be sure of maintaining the rental value.

Each of the potential remedies will be considered in turn, and it is necessary to begin by considering the chief restriction on mid-term dilapidations claims, which is the *Leasehold Property (Repairs) Act 1938*.

Leasehold Property (Repairs) Act 1938

The 1938 Act was enacted to deter landlords from pursuing tenants for minor disrepair. Where the Act applies, a landlord who wishes either to forfeit a lease or claim damages, in reliance on breach of a tenant's repairing obligation, must first serve a notice under *s. 146, Law of Property Act 1925*. The notice must contain specified wording to bring to the tenant's attention its rights under the 1938 Act. The tenant then has 28 days in which to serve a counternotice, claiming the benefit of the Act – this is something which can be done quickly, easily and inexpensively, and it can be assumed that any tenant will do so. That prevents the landlord from claiming damages or forfeiting the lease without the court's permission, and permission can only be granted on one of five statutory grounds, which are broadly directed at ensuring that the disrepair is sufficiently significant. Those grounds are:

a) *"That the immediate remedying of the breach is requisite for preventing substantial diminution in the value of the landlord's reversion, or that the value thereof has already been substantially diminished by the breach*

b) *That the immediate remedying of the breach is required for giving effect in relation to the premises to the purposes of any enactment, or of any byelaw or other provision having effect under an enactment, or for giving effect to any order of the court or requirement of any authority under any such enactment or any such byelaw or other provision as aforesaid*

c) *Where the lessee is not in occupation of the whole of the premises as respects which the covenant or agreement is proposed to be enforced, that the immediate remedying of the breach is required in the interests of the occupier of those premises or of part thereof*

d) *That the breach can be immediately remedied at an expense that is relatively small in comparison with the much greater expense that would probably be occasioned by postponement of the necessary work*

e) *Special circumstances exist which in the opinion of the court render it just and equitable that leave should be given"*

It used to be thought that on an application for permission under the Act the landlord need only make out a *prima facie* case that one of the five grounds was satisfied, and that full investigation of the applicable ground would await the trial of the landlord's substantive claim. *Associated British Ports v CH Bailey [1990] 2 AC 704* established that the normal civil standard of proof applies, hence an application is likely to have to go to a full trial. In order to enforce the repairing obligation, therefore, the landlord has to incur the expense, delay and litigation risk of two trials instead of one. This is an effective deterrent, and applications under the Act are unusual.

The Act applies to tenancies granted for seven years or more, so long as there are three or more years of the term remaining. Therefore, it has been usual for landlords to wait to deal with disrepair until the last three years of the lease, and typically at the end of the lease.

The average length of new lease being granted currently is around five or six years, and so there are many new leases to which the Act does not apply. With such a short term, though, landlords are still usually prepared to put off dealing with disrepair until the end of the lease, since there may not be much deterioration in the fabric of a property over a period of a few years. Also, at the end of the lease there is better information over the likely immediate future of the property, which is relevant to assessing damages. Whether at that time the tenant intends to take a new lease, whether redevelopment appears a good option, whether upgrading is needed, whether an incoming tenant would pay less because of any disrepair, are all factors which will affect the landlord's actions, and its legal remedies.

Damages

The *Leasehold Property (Repairs) Act 1938* is the principal reason for not bringing a damages claim for disrepair in mid-term, but there are others.

When a claim is brought in mid-term, the measure of damages is generally the amount by which the value of the landlord's reversionary interest has been diminished by the breach of repairing covenant (*Doe d.*

Worcester School Trustees v Rowlands (1841) 9 C & P 734). There is a suggestion in the judgment of Lord Herschell in the House of Lords' decision in *Ebbett v Conquest [1896] AC 490* that there may be circumstances where the cost of repair would be the measure instead, but this has never happened in a decided case, and it is thought that his comment may be explained as suggesting that the cost of repair could sometimes be a good guide to the diminution in value of the reversion.

In any event, the amount of damages awarded could not exceed the diminution in value of the reversion, by reason of provision to that effect in *s.18(1), Landlord and Tenant Act 1927* (which will be considered further in Chapters 6 and 7, in relation to dilapidations at lease-end).

An adverse effect on the value of the reversion may be difficult to prove in mid-term. If there is a significant length of term remaining, placing a value on the landlord's interest at all may require assumptions as to the circumstances which will exist at the end of the term, such as the planning context, the market in the particular type of property, the legislative context, and other matters. There will necessarily be a high degree of uncertainty about such assumptions, and therefore a doubt over the reliability of the valuation. To make a reliable judgment about the effect upon that valuation of any disrepair would be even more problematic.

Even where the residue of the term is not particularly long, though, an obstacle for the landlord will be that any hypothetical purchaser of the landlord's interest would have the benefit of the existing lease, with the rental income, and along with it the benefit of the repairing obligations in the lease. That may make it unconvincing to argue that the value of the reversion has been diminished.

In some situations, establishing diminution may be less of a problem. If the landlord's interest is itself leasehold, and the landlord is subject to repairing obligations owed to a superior landlord, that is plainly a matter which should be taken into account (e.g. *Ebbetts v Conquest [1896] AC 490*). If the tenant's breach of repairing obligation exposes the landlord to potential claims under the *Defective Premises Act 1972*, that would be another factor of obvious relevance to valuation. If the remaining term is short, then the valuation difficulties would be much less, and the questions whether or not the tenancy is within the *Landlord and Tenant Act 1954*, and if so how much rent might be obtainable upon renewal, would also be highly relevant.

In general, though, showing diminution in the value of the reversion is very often a problem in mid-term. It is also true that a successful claim for damages does not result in a property which has been repaired. If the landlord has no right to enter and do work itself, it cannot spend the damages received on carrying out repairs until the end of the term. When the impact of the *Leasehold Property (Repairs) Act 1938* is taken into account as well, it is understandable that mid-term damages claims are few and far between.

Specific performance

The House of Lords in *Co-operative Insurance Society Ltd v Argyll Stores (Holdings) Ltd [1998] AC 1* considered at length the reasons why specific performance is almost never granted to compel a tenant to comply with a repairing covenant.

The case was actually concerned, not with disrepair, but with breach of a covenant, standard in retail developments, that the tenant should remain open for trade during the normal opening hours of the development. The tenant had a lease of a food superstore, and was trading at a loss. Having failed to find an assignee or undertenant to relieve them of their lease liabilities, and having failed to persuade the landlord to accept a surrender of the lease, they simply closed the premises. This was a plain breach of covenant, as the tenant acknowledged. Neither forfeiture of the lease, nor payment of damages, would have represented a good outcome for the landlord, who needed the store to be trading, as an important generator of footfall within the development. They therefore sought specific performance to enforce the covenant.

The sanctions for breach of an order for specific performance (committal, fine, sequestration of assets) are such that the court is concerned that a defendant should be left in no doubt as to what it must do to comply. This is usually straightforward in the case of prohibitory injunctions, in a negative form, e.g. not to cut down a neighbour's leylandii hedge. Mandatory orders can present more difficulties of definition.

In this context there was scope for argument as to whether the tenant could sufficiently comply with the keep-open covenant by, for example, opening the roller shutter and putting one employee on the tobacconist's kiosk; or by operating with half the usual staff, selling a reduced range of goods, failing to promote the store, and failing to keep it repaired, clean and tidy.

These points were considered by way of analogy with enforcement of repairing obligations. In the case of building works it can be all but impossible to define with sufficient precision the nature and extent of the works, building materials and methods to be used. An item in a specification of works reading 're-render flank wall' might be sufficient for a tender, or a quote, or perhaps for a damages claim. For a defendant wanting to know what it must do to avoid the risk of committal to prison, however, many questions might remain. Must I re-render all of the wall, even though a third of the existing render is sound? What materials should I use? Must I redecorate afterwards? With what colour and quality of paint? How many coats?

In the event of failure to agree, the only safe solution would be to return to court for guidance, perhaps repeatedly. Not only is that an unsatisfactory way to conduct a commercial endeavour, it also places the court in a supervisory role to which it is unsuited.

Specific performance has been granted on rare occasions: in *Rainbow Estates Ltd v Tokenhold [1999] Ch 64* specific performance represented the only effective sanction open to the landlord, in the absence of a forfeiture clause or 'self-help' clause in the lease. The judge said:

> "...*there is great need for caution in granting the remedy against a tenant, but also ... it will be a rare case in which the remedy of specific performance will be the appropriate one: in the case of commercial leases, the landlord will normally have the right to forfeit or to enter and do the repairs at the expense of the tenant*".

It is generally a safe assumption that specific performance will not be granted, and in practice landlords very rarely seek to enforce repairing obligations in this way. A recent example was *Zinc Cobham 1 Ltd v Adda Hotels [2018] EWHC 1025 (Ch)*, in which the landlord sought specific performance of repairing obligations, to force its tenant to spend more than £100m to rectify breaches of covenant requiring it to carry on trade in 10 Hilton-branded hotels in accordance with Hilton's operating standards. The landlord claimed that the condition of the hotels had reduced the value of its reversionary interests and, because it would be very difficult to quantify the compensation needed to make good its loss, an award of damages would not provide it with an adequate remedy.

The tenant applied to strike out the landlord's claim. The landlord accepted that to order specific performance of the tenant's principal trading obligations would be to require it to carry on an activity, and this would only be ordered in exceptional circumstances. However, it argued, what it sought was an order for specific performance of obligations relating to the *way* in which it traded, which was an order requiring the tenant to achieve a result, and which was permissible.

The court considered that the landlord's application had an air of unreality about it. If an order could not be granted for specific performance of the tenant's principal trading obligations, it followed that the court could not grant an order in relation to the ancillary obligations relating to the mode of trading. An order for specific performance would in any event be difficult to supervise and the only enforcement mechanism available would be contempt of court, which would be oppressive.

The landlord had not shown that it had a legitimate interest that extended beyond pecuniary compensation. It had accepted that completion of the work would make no difference to the rents payable under the leases, totalling £26m. Furthermore, the alleged difficulties in valuation were more imaginary than real. And even if the valuation exercise were to be as difficult as had been suggested, that would not be a reason to award specific performance in place of the usual remedy for breach of contract, which sounds in damages (*Morris-Garner v One Step (Support) Ltd [2018] UKSC 20*).

Any damages payable would be less than the cost of the work and it would be inequitable to require the tenant to spend a sum that would far exceed the landlord's likely loss. A pecuniary award would provide the landlord with an adequate remedy and, because there was no real prospect of obtaining an order for specific performance at trial, the landlord's claim was struck out.

Coincidentally, Hilton was also involved in *Blue Manchester Ltd v North West Ground Rents Ltd [2019] EWHC 142 (TCC)*, which demonstrates that specific performance remains available in appropriate cases. This case is considered for completeness, though it departs somewhat from the subject-matter of this book, being concerned with enforcement of a landlord's repairing obligation by a tenant.

The case concerned Beetham Tower in Manchester. The tower is 47 storeys high, and 23 floors of it are let to Blue Manchester, owner of the Hilton Hotel, on a 999-year lease. There is a serious issue with the sealant holding together the glass panels of the building, and temporary 'stitch plates' have been installed to keep the glass in place. No more permanent solution has yet been implemented, and Hilton was concerned both about safety, and about the visual impact of the stitch plates. Under the lease the landlord was obliged to keep the façade *"in good and substantial repair and when necessary … reinstate, replace and renew it."* There was also a reverse Jervis v Harris clause, allowing the tenant to undertake works at the landlord's cost in the event of default.

The judge was prepared to order specific performance of the landlord's repairing obligation, the proposed solution being the installation of an alternative glazed facing representing a like-for-like replacement of the existing glazing units (no specification for the remedial work existed, however). The stitch plates were designed to last no longer than three years, leading the judge to conclude that the landlord had not discharged its obligation. He also considered that aesthetic standards could be relevant, and that there would have to have been a compelling reason for the tenant to be required to accept the unattractive stitch plates as a permanent solution.

In the circumstances, the judge considered that damages were an inadequate remedy, and further that it would not be satisfactory to leave the tenant to carry out the repairs and recover the costs from the landlord. The landlord was allowed 18 months to repair the building and restore it to substantially the same external appearance as at the date of the lease. However, if the costs were to be disproportionate, the landlord might apply for approval to a different remedial scheme.

Subsequently, in *Blue Manchester Ltd v North West Ground Rents Ltd [2020] EWHC 2777 (TCC)*, the landlord did apply for such approval, though the court considered that it ought not to revisit the merits of the original decision, and force the claimant to accept what it regarded as the lesser option. However, an extension of time was allowed.

Apart from the unusual nature of the property concerned, and the obvious risk posed by the potential for sheets of glass to fall many storeys into the street, it may be suggested that tenants have a greater chance of success in enforcing a landlord's repairing obligation by specific performance than the other way around. First, a tenant is more likely to be concerned with a specific operational problem, such as a leaking roof (or a failing glass façade), which allows the court to characterise the claim as one designed to require the defendant to achieve a result, rather than carry on an activity. Secondly, courts are perhaps more inclined to sympathise with a tenant.

Declaration

In *Office Depot International (UK) Ltd v UBS Asset Management [2018] EWHC 1494 (TCC)* the court declined to grant a declaration as to what repair works were required. The tenant held a 20-year lease of a building, but required, some years in advance of lease expiry, guidance as to what works, if any, were needed to put the property into a state which complied with the repairing obligation. This was principally because of limitation issues arising from collateral warranties given by the building contractor. There was no dispute as to the meaning of the repair covenant.

The court declined a declaration because:

- There was no dispute as to the scope of works required. The choice of works required to maintain and repair the property was for the tenant, and it was not open to the tenant to require the landlord to identify or agree any particular scheme of works.

- The tenant did not put forward a positive case as to what was required to be done, and it was not for the court to assume responsibility for how the contract was to be performed.

- It would not be appropriate for the court to carry out an inquisitorial process to identify the required works. The dilapidations claim had not crystallised, and the tenant only put forward neutral expert schemes without adopting any of them.

- While the court could adjudicate on whether the covenant had been performed, in the event of dispute, it could not supervise performance of the covenant.

This decision appears to close down a potential option for tenants whose break option is conditional upon compliance with repairing obligations. Whether a landlord would fare any better must be doubtful. The point that it is for the tenant to identify remedial works would apply with greater force, so that the most a landlord might hope to achieve would probably be a declaration as to (a) the existence of specific items of disrepair, and (b) the tenant's liability to put them right. A landlord going to the trouble of establishing those two things might as well do so in the context of seeking damages or forfeiture; remedies which would actually have the effect of enforcing the tenant's repair covenants.

Summary

The *Leasehold Property (Repairs) Act 1938* places procedural obstacles in the way of enforcing repairing obligations by means of forfeiture of the lease or a claim for damages. It requires the landlord to prove one of five statutory grounds which establish that the disrepair complained of is significant, and not trivial. It is an effective deterrent, and discourages damages claims or forfeiture in relation to disrepair. It only applies to leases granted for seven years or more, and ceases to apply in the last three years of the term.

Damages claims are in any event problematic in mid-term due to evidential difficulties in showing that the value of the landlord's interest has been diminished as a result of the disrepair.

The courts only rarely grant specific performance of tenants' repairing obligations, because of the difficulty in specifying exactly what the tenant must do to comply.

It appears that it may be difficult also to obtain a declaration from the court as to what repairs are required.

CHAPTER FOUR

MID-TERM DILAPIDATIONS (2) – FORFEITURE, JERVIS V HARRIS CLAIMS AND OTHER MATTERS

Content

This chapter outlines further available remedies for addressing breach of repairing obligation during the term of a lease: forfeiture, the Jervis v Harris claim, and other means by which the landlord may exert pressure.

Forfeiture

In the previous chapter we considered the problems in the way of mid-term claims for damages or specific performance; in this chapter we begin by considering another little-used remedy, at least in relation to disrepair: namely, forfeiture of the lease. Although comparatively uncommon, there may be circumstances in which forfeiture is really the only satisfactory way of dealing with persistent and serious default. Of course, the *Leasehold Property (Repairs) Act 1938* is an important reason why forfeiture is little-used in relation to disrepair. The general nature and features of forfeiture as a remedy give rise to additional reasons.

What is forfeiture?

Forfeiture simply means termination of the lease by the landlord, for some default by the tenant. Forfeiture also terminates any interests granted out of the lease, such as sub-leases or charges. The Law Commission has criticised the existing law of forfeiture severely, as being over-complex, archaic and not always coherent. The Commission's draft Termination of Tenancies Bill was first published in 1994, and republished after a further consultation in 2006. It proposes abolishing the law of forfeiture completely, to replace it with a new statutory scheme. It is to be hoped that the proposals will be enacted in due course.

Nature of the right to forfeit

There is no implied right to forfeit; it is a creature of contract. Forfeiture provisions are sometimes referred to as 're-entry' provisions, or as 'provisos for re-entry', and they may be drafted in terms of the landlord re-entering upon the premises, rather than forfeiting the lease. This is simply archaic terminology, and the effect of the provision is the same.

They tend to be in fairly standard form, and entitle the landlord to forfeit:

- When the tenant has been in arrears for a certain period (usually 7, 14 or 21 days – commonly referred to as a 'grace period')

- If the tenant is in breach of any other tenant's covenant in the lease (it is this ground of forfeiture which is relevant in the case of dilapidations, of course)

- If the tenant has entered into an insolvency procedure.

Where a right to forfeit arises, the effect is not to terminate the lease, but to confer on the landlord a right to do so if it chooses. The lease is voidable at the landlord's option.

How is forfeiture effected?

To forfeit the lease, the landlord must do something which demonstrates an unequivocal intention to bring the lease to an end. There are two ways of doing that: (a) peaceable re-entry, and (b) serving proceedings claiming possession.

Peaceable re-entry

Peaceable re-entry involves securing the property physically, without to court. In the case of a building, this is usually a matter of changing the locks. The forfeiture clause will usually provide that the landlord can 're-enter part in the name of the whole'.

The courts have tended to frown on peaceable re-entry in recent years. In *Billson v Residential Apartments Ltd [1992] 1 AC 494*, the House of Lords described it as "*a sure recipe for violence*". Nevertheless, it remains in use by landlords, as it can be quicker, cheaper and more effective than court proceedings. It also has the advantage that the landlord immediately becomes the owner of any items found on the premises which would have otherwise have been tenant's fixtures (*Re Palmiero: Debtor 3666 of 1999 [1999] 3 EGLR 27*).

There is a risk of committing criminal offences when forfeiting by peaceable re-entry:

- under *s.1(2), Protection from Eviction Act 1977*, where the premises are "*let as a dwelling*" (or comprise both commercial and residential elements, see *Patel v Pirabakaran [2006] EWCA Civ 685*); and

- under *s.6, Criminal Law Act 1977*, if force against the person or property is used in recovering possession of any premises (not just residential ones), so long as there is a person present on the premises who is opposed to the landlord recovering possession.

Peaceable re-entry is therefore used only on commercial premises, and usually out of business hours, often over a weekend or early in the morning, when it can be expected that no-one will be present.

It is less likely to be used in relation to breach of repairing covenant than in some other situations, because there is likely to be dispute on many detailed questions of fact, which are best resolved in the context of proceedings.

Forfeiture by proceedings

Forfeiture by proceedings, by contrast, presents fewer complications. However, once proceedings have been served, the choice to forfeit is irrevocable, and the lease cannot be restored by, for example, the landlord discontinuing its claim. The status of the lease after that date up to judgment is uncertain, and depends on the outcome of the proceedings.

- Should the landlord's claim be dismissed, the lease has never been forfeited.

- If relief from forfeiture is granted so that the lease is reinstated, that is retrospective to the start of proceedings.

- If the court makes an order for possession, the lease is forfeit as of the start of proceedings.

The period of uncertainty from the start of proceedings to the date of the court's order is known as the 'twilight period', and estate management can be complicated during that period, since the landlord cannot enforce the tenant's obligations (*Associated Deliveries v Harrison (1985) 50 P&CR 91*).

Section 146, Law of Property Act 1925

Apart from a few exceptions (principally when forfeiting for non-payment of rent), where a landlord intends to forfeit a lease, it cannot do so unless it has first served on the tenant a notice under *s.146, Law of Property Act 1925* (a 's.146 notice'). This is a warning notice which specifies the breach of covenant complained of, requires the tenant to remedy it, and requires the tenant to pay compensation for it. In the dilapidations context, where the *Leasehold Property (Repairs) Act 1938* applies, the notice must additionally contain prominent wording notifying the tenant of its rights under the Act.

The notice will inform the tenant that the landlord intends to forfeit the lease if the breach is not remedied within a reasonable time. What is a reasonable time is of course fact-dependent; in the case of a significant programme of repair work, the period may be months or more.

Waiver of the right to forfeit

One of the more problematic aspects of the law of forfeiture generally is the ease with which the right to forfeit may be waived. Once a landlord has acquired knowledge of the facts giving rise to a right to forfeit, he is put to his election whether or not to allow the lease to continue, and any act or statement after then which expressly or implicitly acknowledges the continuing existence of the lease will be taken as a choice to allow it to continue, and will waive the right to forfeit.

The requisite knowledge, and also the act of waiver, need not be that of the landlord itself, but might be that of an agent, solicitor or somebody else involved in the management of the property for the landlord, such as a resident caretaker. Hence waiver may take place without the landlord itself ever knowing of the right to forfeit, or doing anything to waive it. Quite a slender acknowledgement of the continuing existence of the lease may potentially suffice as a waiver, such as an incautious reference in correspondence to 'your lease', so that it is very easy for the right to forfeit to be lost inadvertently.

The law makes a distinction between 'continuing' and 'once-and-for-all' breaches of covenant, in relation to the operation of waiver. In the case of a continuing breach, a fresh right to forfeit arises immediately after each act of waiver, and the landlord does not need to serve a fresh s.146 notice. Generally speaking, breach of the covenant regulating the use of the property, and breach of the covenant to keep in repair, are considered to be continuing breaches.

It follows, therefore, that waiver of the right to forfeit is not generally a concern in dilapidations cases. However, the Court of Appeal has expressed some doubt over whether a fresh s.146 notice need be served following an act of waiver in relation to a continuing breach (*Farimani v Gates [1984] 2 EGLR 66*), and a cautious landlord might still be very mindful of not waiving the right to forfeit until such time as forfeiture has been effected, which means not accepting any rent during that time. This may be a lengthy period, if the disrepair requires substantial remedial work.

Relief from forfeiture

Relief from forfeiture can be thought of conveniently as reinstatement of the lease, though it may not take that form. Though relief was originally granted under the court's inherent equitable jurisdiction, there has been significant statutory intervention since then, and there are a variety of jurisdictions under which the court may relieve tenants, sub-tenants and chargees from forfeiture, with different rules applying to each.

In the case of forfeiture on the ground of breach of repairing covenant, the relevant jurisdiction for the tenant to claim relief is that arising under *s.146(2), Law of Property Act 1925*; if it is a sub-tenant or chargee who applies for relief, then the jurisdiction arises under *s.146(4)*.

An application for relief can be made immediately following service by the landlord of a s.146 notice; it is not necessary to wait until the landlord has actually forfeited. This is sometimes done where the landlord is thought to be likely to forfeit by peaceable re-entry, as the pending relief application may dissuade the landlord from proceeding in that way.

Application cannot be made after the landlord has enforced its order for possession; if the landlord has peaceably re-entered, there is no set time limit, but the application must be made promptly (*Billson v Residential Apartments Ltd [1992] 1 AC 494*).

As a general principle, an applicant must remedy all breaches of covenant in order to obtain relief. Ordinarily this means that in a repair case, the applicant will be required to carry out the remedial work, within a timescale laid down by the court. However, this is not an inflexible rule, and it may be that relief could be granted without that requirement, in a case where the court is satisfied that the works would be of no real benefit to anybody (*Associated British Ports v CH Bailey Plc [1990] 2 AC 703*), or perhaps where some other special circumstances would make it inequitable to impose that requirement.

Pros and cons of forfeiture for disrepair

Forfeiture, in the dilapidations context, is typically undertaken for one of two reasons: (a) the landlord genuinely wishes to recover possession; or (b) the landlord intends that forfeiture should prompt the tenant to make an application for relief, and therefore to remedy the disrepair.

If the intention is to recover possession, the obvious snag is that there may be an application for relief from forfeiture, and this is likely to be successful, so long as the disrepair is remedied. If, on the other hand, the intention is to forfeit as a persuasive measure, the risk for the landlord is that it is an irrevocable step. The tenant may accept the forfeiture, not apply for relief, and abandon the premises. The landlord will be left with a property which is not only still in disrepair, but also vacant.

Vacant commercial property is increasingly a headache for landlords, for a number of reasons:

- Most obviously, a vacant property is not producing income; there will be a rental void before another tenant can be found, and letting expenses.

- The insurance cost will fall on the landlord, and insurers' security requirements will have to be complied with. Whatever their requirements, the landlord will want to keep the property secure, and this may cost.

- If the premises are part of a larger property, e.g. a shopping mall, there will be an unrecoverable part of the service expenditure in relation to the vacant unit.

- Business rates will be payable on the empty property, subject to available reliefs.

- Once the lease has been forfeited, any guarantors or former tenants who may be liable on the lease covenants will be released.

- Utilities suppliers are likely to terminate their contracts with the tenant, and deemed supply contracts with the landlord may come into effect instead, under which the landlord may face hefty estimated demands.

- The landlord becomes a bailee of any tenant's goods found on the premises, and this is often a practical problem. The landlord must give the tenant access to collect its goods at any reasonable time, and often cannot dispose of the goods without serving on the tenant a notice under the *Torts (Interference With Goods) Act 1977*.

A landlord who proposes to go down the forfeiture route should have weighed these consequences, and be prepared to recover possession. If that is not an acceptable outcome, remedies other than forfeiture should be considered.

Forfeiture on the basis of disrepair will require service of a s.146 notice, following which the landlord must wait for a reasonable time, potentially several months, before actually forfeiting. During that period, the landlord may consider it prudent not to accept rent, so as to avoid any necessity to serve a fresh s.146 notice, so several months' income may be in jeopardy. Forfeiture is likely to be effected by court proceedings, not peaceable re-entry, and that brings with it all the usual considerations of expense, delay and litigation risk. Those factors are doubled if it has first been necessary to obtain permission to forfeit under the *Leasehold Property (Repairs) Act 1938*.

Despite all these disadvantages, forfeiture may be the only effective remedy in a case of long-standing and serious disrepair, with a lengthy residue of lease term remaining, and a history of inaction by the tenant.

Jervis v Harris claims

So far we have identified significant difficulties in relation to mid-term action by way of damages claims, specific performance, and forfeiture. In the event of a landlord opting to deal with dilapidations mid-term, it is likely that they will proceed instead by means of what is usually called a 'Jervis v Harris claim'. The ability to use this procedure depends entirely on the terms of the lease; provisions in leases giving landlords this option were first introduced as a means of circumventing the *Leasehold Property (Repairs) Act 1938*. However, landlords may use this procedure whether or not the 1938 Act applies, so long as the provision is there in the lease, and it is increasingly in use as an alternative to leaving disrepair to be dealt with by a damages claim at the end of the lease (or perhaps as a preparatory step, with a subsequent terminal dilapidations claim in mind).

The basic structure of a Jervis v Harris clause is as follows:

- The landlord has a right to enter the property and inspect its physical condition.

- It may then serve a notice detailing any disrepair and requiring the tenant to remedy it.

- The tenant is then under an obligation either to carry out the work within a certain period or, depending on the terms of the clause, to start the work within a certain period and then 'proceed diligently' to complete it.

- If the tenant fails to do so, the landlord has a right to enter the property and carry out the repair work itself.

- The cost of doing the work is recoverable from the tenant.

The reason why this procedure circumvents the 1938 Act is that the claim for the cost of the work is a claim for debt, while the Act applies only to forfeiture and damages. There was for a long time an uncertainty over this, and conflicting first-instance decisions, although the weight of opinion favoured the view that it was a claim for debt. The uncertainty meant that a landlord who went down the 'repair notice' route took a significant risk: if the landlord were to do the work and claim the cost, and the court were to hold that the clause was ineffective to get around the 1938 Act, then the landlord would be unable to correct matters by following the procedure under the Act, because there would be no disrepair at that time (*SEDAC Investments v Tanner [1982] 1 WLR 1342*). The doubt was eventually resolved by the Court of Appeal in *Jervis v Harris [1996] Ch 195*, which explains why these claims are referred to as above.

A further consequence of this type of claim being regarded as a debt claim, is that there is no statutory cap on the amount recoverable, by way of contrast to a damages claim, where the amount is capped by *s.18(1), Landlord and Tenant Act 1927*.

The Jervis v Harris claim is not problem-free:

- The landlord's right to enter to do the work, and subsequently to recover the cost, is predicated entirely upon the work in question being identified in the repair notice (in practical terms the notice will usually be accompanied by a detailed schedule of dilapidations). It is almost invariably the case that as a programme of works progresses, it becomes apparent that the disrepair is in some respects more extensive than at first identified, or that some fresh item of work requires to be done. If the landlord proceeds to do work which is not identified in the notice, that is technically a trespass, and might be restrained by injunction. Serving a fresh notice, and putting the original scheduled works on hold while waiting for the notice period to elapse, is likely to be impractical. It may equally be the case that simply leaving the new work undone is impractical. What will probably happen is that the landlord will proceed with the new work, but be unable to recover the cost.

- The tenant is unlikely to be happy about the landlord entering the premises, possibly closing them down for several weeks, in order to do the repair work. It may allege breach of quiet enjoyment covenant, and seek an injunction to prevent the landlord doing the work; or, it may be the landlord who seeks an injunction to compel the tenant to permit entry. Either way, the court will balance the inconvenience as between the parties, and may well decide not to permit the landlord to enter, as it did in *Hammersmith & Fulham LBC v Creska [2000] L&TR 288*.

- Even if the landlord carries out the work without any of these problems, and sends the tenant the bill, the landlord is exposed as to the amount of its expenditure. The tenant may argue that some of the work was not within its repairing obligation, or that the landlord has incorrectly identified some items of disrepair, or that the landlord spent too much on the work, or improved the premises. It is highly likely that the claim will be reduced to some extent.

The reason why Jervis v Harris claims are increasingly popular despite these drawbacks, is that they only present as problems if the landlord gets to the stage of actually doing the work itself. This is unusual; the normal course of events is that service of the notice prompts a negotiation, and that the tenant ends up agreeing to do at least some of the scheduled work. So the procedure may be used as an interim measure, to limit the disrepair which will exist at lease expiry. Alternatively, the landlord who anticipates that *s.18(1), Landlord and Tenant Act 1927* is likely to limit a damages claim significantly may go through the Jervis v Harris procedure near the end of the lease in substitution for a terminal dilapidations claim; that requires careful timing to ensure that the landlord is in a position, if required, to finish the work and claim the cost from the tenant prior to lease expiry.

Other means of applying pressure

Without exercising any of the above formal remedies, or in conjunction with them, landlords may have other talking-points when it comes to persuading tenants to comply with their repairing obligations.

Applications for landlord's consent

Landlord's consent may be required for any number of things under leases: assignment, underletting, change of use, alterations, applications for planning consent, and others. Landlords are sometimes prone to use an application for consent to try to resolve outstanding management issues in relation to the lease, and to indicate that consent will be forthcoming only upon condition that the tenant carries out repairs, or reinstates alterations, or some other such matter.

Generally speaking, this is not permissible. The main types of consent application (assignment, underletting, alterations) are subject to implied provisos that the landlord should not unreasonably withhold consent, or impose unreasonable conditions (*s.19(1)-(2), Landlord and Tenant Act 1927*), and it is very likely that the lease will make express provision to that effect anyway. In the case of assignment and underletting, the tenant may claim damages from the landlord if it does act unreasonably (*s.4, Landlord and Tenant Act 1988*). The caselaw establishes that it is unreasonable for the landlord to use applications for consent so as to gain a 'collateral advantage', that is, to enhance or increase the rights given by the lease. The landlord has its remedies for breaches of covenant under the lease, and to use an application for consent to hold the tenant to ransom in relation to breaches of covenant is effectively to claim an additional remedy. To do so would therefore be regarded as trying to gain a collateral advantage, and would accordingly be unreasonable.

As regards breach of repairing covenant, or related matters such as reinstatement of alterations, the general rule is therefore that an outstanding breach of covenant will not be regarded as a sufficient reason to refuse consent (*Beale v Worth [1993] EGCS 135; Farr v Ginnings [1928] 44 TLR 249*). A good modern example is provided by *Singh v Dhanji [2014] EWCA Civ 414*. In that case, the landlord tried to make it a condition of granting consent to an assignment that the tenant should reinstate some alterations which had been carried out in breach of covenant, at a cost of some £140,000. That was held to be unreasonable. There is the odd example from case-law in which the state of disrepair of the premises has been sufficiently serious to justify refusal (e.g. *Goldstein v Sanders [1915] 1 Ch 549*, where the condition of the property was described as "little short of outrageous"), but it is hard to draw any clear idea from the decided cases of how serious it needs to be.

If the landlord can show that a refusal of consent, or the imposition of a condition, is necessary to prevent his rights under the lease from being significantly prejudiced, then that may amount to a reasonable basis for refusing consent. An example might be where a tenant who is a good covenant, but who is in default of a repairing obligation, wants to assign to a much weaker covenant who is less likely to be able to meet the obligations at the end of the lease. *Orlando Investments Ltd v Grosvenor Estate (Belgravia) [1989] 43 EG 175* was an example where the breaches of covenant were substantial and long-standing, and the landlord had reasonable grounds to be concerned that the assignee would not address them. It was held to be reasonable to refuse consent. But if the assignee is just as good a covenant, or if the breach is not serious and can be just as easily dealt with by the assignee, the landlord is going to be in difficulties.

Opposing renewal of lease

While opposition to renewal of a lease within *Part II* of the *Landlord and Tenant Act 1954* is clearly not something which arises mid-term, the potential for opposition may assist in persuading a tenant to address disrepair. Among the statutory grounds on which a landlord may oppose the grant of a new lease is the following, contained in *s.30(1)(a)*:

> "*Where under the current tenancy the tenant has any obligations as respects the repair and maintenance of the holding, that the tenant ought not to be granted a new tenancy in view of the state of repair of the holding, being a state resulting from the tenant's failure to comply with the said obligations*".

The particular merit of opposing renewal on a 'tenant default' ground such as this is that if successful, no compensation is payable to the tenant upon the termination of their tenancy.

The prospect of losing the premises, without compensation, may have persuasive value.

Challenging operation of break option

We will be considering in the next chapter the relevance of repairing and related obligations to the operation of tenant's break options. For present purposes, it may be said briefly that where an option is conditional upon the tenant having complied with its repair obligations, this can present tenants with a significant uncertainty as regards the operation of the break, and potentially significant expenditure in repair works if they are to maximise the chances of operating the break successfully.

That gives landlords another lever for exerting pressure on tenants to put property in repair. If repairs would cost £150,000, but exercising the break would save future rental liability of £500,000, the tenant should be amenable to persuasion, unless they have taken a firm decision not to operate the break.

Summary

Forfeiture of the lease, even in circumstances where the *Leasehold Property (Repairs) Act 1938* does not apply, offers uncertainty as to either gaining possession, or forcing the tenant to comply with the repairing covenant. It should only be undertaken where the landlord is prepared to recover possession.

Perhaps the most effective remedy, generally speaking, is the 'repair notice' procedure under *Jervis v Harris*, whereby the landlord may be entitled to do repair work itself, and recover the cost from the tenant. This remedy brings with it practical difficulties where the landlord actually proceeds to do the work, but it is very often possible to negotiate a programme of works to be undertaken by the tenant instead.

There may be additional levers which the landlord can use to exert pressure on the tenant to carry out repairs: withholding consent to an assignment, threatening to oppose renewal of the lease when it expires, or failure to comply with the conditions for exercise of a break option.

CHAPTER FIVE

CONDITIONAL TENANT'S BREAK OPTIONS AND THE PHYSICAL STATE OF THE PROPERTY

Content

This chapter considers how breach of repairing, decorating and reinstatement obligations, and the related matter of failure to give vacant possession, can defeat the tenant's exercise of any break option contained in its lease.

Another matter which can arise before expiry of the full lease term, and which raises issues relating to the physical condition of the property, is exercise of a tenant's break option.

A break option is simply a right to bring a lease to an end ahead of what would otherwise be the expiry date, by serving a notice. A lease might be granted for a term of ten years, for example, but with a right to terminate it halfway through, at the end of the fifth year. A break option may be operable only by the tenant, or only by the landlord, or it may be mutual.

Tenant's break options serve many purposes:

- Most obviously, they give useful flexibility as regards the length of the lease commitment.

- Sometimes a break option is linked to a rent review, so that the tenant has the ability to walk away from the property if it is unhappy with the level of the reviewed rent.

- Break options may be used as a means of compromising between the differing ambitions of landlord and tenant for the term length; this has been increasingly common over the past 25 to 30 years, with the downward trend in the length of lease terms.

- In some retail leases, the rent payable is calculated upon a formula based on the tenant's turnover, and it is common for such leases to contain a mutual break option; in that way, either party may terminate the lease if the anticipated level of turnover has not been achieved after the first few years.

A tenant's option to break is very often conditional on compliance with obligations in the lease, and this can give landlords an opportunity to try to frustrate the break, as they may be particularly inclined to do in a falling rental market.

Compliance with repair covenants

This has historically been one of the most common areas of contention; it is likely that the relevant condition will be one requiring compliance with all covenants, but it is compliance with the repair obligation which presents tenants with the greatest difficulties.

The *RICS Professional Statement: Code of Practice for Leasing Business Premises* recommends that tenant's break options should not be conditional upon compliance with repairing covenants, since landlords have plenty of other remedies for disrepair. However, it should be acknowledged that disrepair is an entirely proper concern for landlords. In return for granting a valuable property right, the right to break, they might quite reasonably expect to get the property back in a lettable condition. The problem lies, not in the principle, but in the way in which the courts have interpreted these conditions.

In *Finch v Underwood (1876) 2 Ch D 310*, Mellish LJ observed:

> *"In a case like this, if a tenant wishes to claim the benefit of such a covenant he should send in his surveyor to see what repairs are needed and should effect the repairs which the surveyor certifies to be requisite. The court would be inclined to give credit to a survey thus honestly*

made, and would lean towards holding the condition precedent to have been complied with".

Despite that apparently accommodating approach, the disrepair in that case, which would only have cost between £13 and £45 to put right (admittedly in Victorian money), was sufficient to defeat the option.

That passage from *Finch v Underwood* has been quoted with approval in many cases since, right up to the present day, and yet despite tenants following the advice contained in it, break options are regularly defeated by what appear to be minor matters. In *Sirhowy Investments v Henderson [2014] EWHC 3562 (Ch)*, the exercise of the tenants' break option was defeated because they had mended a wooden fence in some places with sheeting panels, instead of restoring it in the original form.

Conditionality on repair has been less of a feature of the caselaw over recent years, perhaps because tenants are getting better at negotiating break clauses. Where a break option is conditional upon repair, it is now common to see the condition qualified to require only 'reasonable', 'substantial' or 'material' compliance.

A condition requiring 'reasonable' compliance was considered in *Gardner v Blaxill [1960] 2 All ER 457*, and the court held that the word *"meant that the tenant could exercise his option provided that he behaved during the tenancy in a way which a reasonably minded tenant might well behave"*. But performance over the whole term is relevant to that assessment, so a breach might defeat the break even though it had been remedied (*Bassett v Whiteley (1982) 45 P&CR 87*). In *Commercial Union v Label Ink [2001] L&TR 380*, it was held that the effect of the word 'reasonably' was that while the tenant did not have to comply fully with the covenants, it did need to show that it had made reasonable efforts to perform them, and it had not.

Another common qualifier is 'material' or 'substantial' compliance. In *Fitzroy House Epworth Street v Financial Times [2006] 2 All ER 776* the two words were considered to be interchangeable. It was held that the standard of compliance required by such a qualification must be assessed by reference to the landlord's ability to re-let or sell the premises without delay or additional expense.

Practical points

The landlord need not prepare a schedule of dilapidations. The tenant's obligation is to keep the property in repair throughout the term, not to react to a schedule. Equally, if a schedule has been served, the tenant should not assume that compliance is defined by reference to the scheduled items. Some disrepair may have been overlooked, or even deliberately omitted. The tenant should do an independent survey as well, as stated in *Finch v Underwood*.

Anecdotally, landlords may find items of disrepair, enabling them to challenge the exercise of break options, by measures such as CCTV drainage surveys. In a whole building lease, the drains will typically be included within the demise, there is often some defect in them, and the tenant is likely to have overlooked them in addressing issues of repair. Tenants should (as always when dealing with disrepair) consider carefully the extent of the demise.

Turning to decorating obligations, they will often require work in the last year of the term, whether or not it is determined early. If so, service by the tenant of a break notice itself creates an obligation to decorate, prior to the break date. *Osborne Assets v Britannia Life (1997)* (*Liverpool County Court, unreported*) is a well-known example of the court holding that the break option had been defeated because the decorating condition had not been complied with. This is a case where the tenant complied to the letter with the *Finch v Underwood* advice, and indeed left the property in a state of repair such that the landlord could not find any fault, upon a visual inspection. However, documentation of the tenant's programme of repairs included a decorator's invoice recording that the interior of the property had been decorated with two coats of paint, instead of the three required by the lease. Courts regard decorating covenants seriously, and non-compliance with them has defeated breaks on several occasions.

Some matters may require landlord's approval, for example paint colours. The tenant should of course seek approval early. If the landlord does not respond (landlords are not obliged to assist tenants to exercise their break options), then the tenant must do the best it can.

Obligations to reinstate alterations may be dependent on the landlord notifying a requirement to reinstate. Most leases do not specify a deadline for the landlord to raise such a requirement, and the current caselaw suggests that in the absence of a time limit, the landlord can raise a valid reinstatement requirement right up to expiry of the term, even where it is clearly far too late for the tenant to be able to comply (e.g. *Scottish Mutual Assurance Society v British Telecommunications Plc (1994) (High Court, unreported)* No reported case on validity of a break option has ever turned on a last-minute reinstatement requirement, but the tenant should ask the landlord's intentions in plenty of time, and stand ready to deal with any late reinstatement requirements as far as possible.

Condition for vacant possession

Another common condition is that vacant possession must be given on the break date. 'Vacant possession' means that (a) the tenant must be out of the premises by the break date, and (b) there is no other impediment to use of the premises by the landlord (e.g. significant quantities of tenant's goods left on the premises).

The *RICS Professional Statement: Code of Practice for Leasing Business Premises* recommends that any condition of this nature should require only that the tenant give up occupation and leave behind no continuing subleases. Although this does not look much different from a requirement to give up vacant possession, it is actually significantly easier to comply with. A condition drafted as per the Code recommendation does not require any consideration of the physical state of the premises; a condition to give up vacant possession does.

A vacant possession condition was considered in *NYK Logistics (UK) Limited v Ibrend Estates BV [2011] 2 P&CR 9*. The break option in that case was not conditional upon the tenant performing its repairing obligations. Nevertheless, a schedule of dilapidations was prepared in the lead-up to lease termination. This was delivered to the tenant less than three weeks before the break date. The tenant arranged to carry out remedial work to the property in the final days leading up to the break date.

It became apparent that it would not be possible to finish the work in time. The parties discussed an arrangement for the vacant possession date to be extended for a week to allow completion of the works, and for the tenant to continue to provide a security presence. The agreement was never finalised, as the approval of the landlord's board was not obtained, but the tenant retained its workmen and security staff on site for some days anyway. The landlord subsequently argued that the break had not operated.

The tenant argued that they had complied with the condition for vacant possession because, had the landlord challenged the continued presence on site, they would simply have withdrawn all personnel immediately. Thus there was no substantial interference with the landlord's enjoyment of possession of the property.

Vacant possession, the Court of Appeal said, means that:

> "…the property is empty of people and that the [landlord] is able to assume and enjoy immediate and exclusive possession, occupation and control of it. It must also be empty of chattels, although the obligation in this respect is likely only to be breached if any chattels left in the property substantially prevent or interfere with the enjoyment of the right of possession of a substantial part of the property."

Since the tenant had people on site beyond the break date, the condition had not been complied with, and the break failed.

The question whether the landlord's enjoyment of possession has been substantially interfered with is limited to the presence of chattels, or potentially tenant's fixtures, at the property. This is where consideration of the physical state of the property becomes relevant, as illustrated by a number of cases in recent years.

Riverside Park Limited v NHS Property Services Limited [2016] EWHC 1313 (Ch)

A tenant sought to exercise its break option in a lease of an office unit. The break option was conditional on the tenant giving vacant possession. The tenant had carried out alterations, including the installation of internal demountable partitioning and those alterations were authorised by a licence to alter. On vacating the premises, the tenant left the partitioning and some other items in the premises. The landlord contended that the break option had not been exercised since the tenant had not given vacant possession.

The court held that the partitions were chattels, since they were merely attached by screws to the raised floor and the suspended ceiling and were not attached to the structure of the building. It was clear that the partitions could be removed without injury to themselves or the fabric of the building.

The court also found that the partitions were, in the words of Lord Greene MR in *Cumberland Consolidated Holdings v Ireland [1946] KB 264*, "*an impediment which substantially prevents or interferes with the right of possession*". As the landlord pointed out, the partitioning had resulted in the creation of a number of small offices in the premises, the effect of which might be described as a 'rabbit warren'.

On this basis, the tenant had failed to give vacant possession and had not triggered its break option.

The court also considered the position if its conclusion that the partitions were chattels was wrong, and they were actually tenant's fixtures. The tenant argued that by virtue of the provisions of the lease and the licence to alter, it was only obliged to remove the works if required to do so by the landlord, and no such requirement had been raised. However, the licence was conditional upon insurers' approval to the alterations having been obtained, and this had never been done. The terms of the licence fell away, therefore: the works were effectively unlicensed and should have been removed. Again, the consequence was that the tenant had failed to give vacant possession.

Secretary of State for Communities and Local Government v South Essex College of Further and Higher Education [2016] PLSCS 249

Commercial premises were let to the defendant tenant, which provided educational services from them. After taking the lease, it had divided them up by erecting partitioning to create an administration area, a server room and six teaching rooms.

When the tenant purported to terminate the tenancy pursuant to a break clause in the lease, the landlord challenged the break on the basis of the failure by the defendant to give *"vacant possession... of the whole of the premises"* on the break date.

The internal partitioning and reception desks remained in place, as did various chattels including computer screens, a photocopier with a sign left on the top reading 'do not move' and a box of student files which the defendant was under a statutory obligation to preserve for audit purposes. The defendant had also left a certain quantity of cabling, wiring, trunking and electrical sockets that related to IT equipment and a telephone system that had previously been in place.

The court held that the tenant had not given vacant possession of the premises on the break date, and accordingly the break had not been validly exercised.

- By leaving the photocopier and the box files in the room, the defendant continued to store goods there and was therefore continuing to make use of the premises after expiry of the break notice.

- Moreover, before the claimant could use the premises, it would have to remove the partitions, reception desks, trunking, cabling and sockets as well as the photocopier and other chattels. Accordingly, the premises were not left in a state in which the claimant could, if it wanted, occupy them without difficulty or objection. There was a substantial impediment to use of a substantial part of the premises.

Capitol Park Leeds v Global Radio Services [2021] EWCA Civ 995

The problem which arose in relation to the 'vacant possession' condition in this case was a novel one. It concerned a three-storey commercial office property in Leeds, let for a term of 24 years from November 2001, but with a tenant's option to break in November 2017.

The break was conditional, among other things, on the tenant giving vacant possession of the Premises, defined so as to include all fixtures and fittings other than tenant's fixtures, and all additions and improvements.

The tenant gave notice to exercise the break, and subsequently carried out a programme of stripping-out works. The parties failed to agree on what elements of the building had formed part of the base build, and what had been installed later, and when it became apparent that a settlement would not be reached, the tenant removed from the building elements including ceiling grids and tiles, fire barriers, floor finishes, windowsills, fan coil units and ductwork, lighting, radiators and pipework.

The landlord claimed that this amounted to a failure to give vacant possession, while the tenant's position was that it might amount to breach of repairing obligation, but not a failure to give vacant possession.

Argument turned on the meaning of "the Premises", with the tenant contending that it meant the premises as they were from time to time, including in their stripped-out condition at the break date. At first instance (*Capitol Park Leeds plc v Global Radio Services Ltd [2020] EWHC 2750 (Ch)*), the court agreed with the landlord that the definition specifically included fixtures, fittings, additions and improvements, precisely so as to ensure that the landlord should not be left with a shell building, which had ramifications for non-compliance with legal obligations, damage to property, insurers' requirements, valuation, and health and safety. The extent of the tenant's strip-out resulted in a physical condition which was a substantial impediment to the landlord's enjoyment of possession of the property, and therefore a failure to give vacant possession.

On appeal it was held that the vacant possession condition was not concerned with the physical state of the unit but with whether the landlord was recovering it free of "*the conventional trilogy of people, chattels and interests*". The condition was not one which required the tenant to have observed and performed their covenants. Moreover, the yield-up covenant *did* require the premises to be yielded up "*in a state of repair condition and decoration which is consistent with the proper performance of the Tenant's covenants*". The fact that the break clause made no mention of repair or condition, when the yield-up covenant did, added support to the tenant's case that the break clause was not concerned with such matters.

The condition therefore required the tenant to return the "Premises" as they were on the break date, free of people, chattels and interests. Whilst the building had been left in a dire state, that did not invalidate the exercise of the break clause. The Court noted that the landlord was not left without a remedy, because it retained its right to damages for breach of covenant.

Settlement

Uncertainty as to the ability to comply with conditions, and perhaps also time pressures, may lead tenants to resolve these issues by means of a cash settlement with the landlord. Operation of a break option therefore potentially represents another trigger for what is effectively recovery of damages by the landlord.

Since it is not actually a damages claim, though, none of the restrictions imposed by the *Leasehold Property (Repairs) Act 1938* or *s.18(1)*, *Landlord and Tenant Act 1927* applies. There is no requirement for the court's permission, and there is no limitation upon the sum recoverable; indeed, there is no 'measure of damages' as such. For the tenant to operate the break successfully, it would have to carry out all outstanding repair work, and landlords can therefore take the cost of repair as a starting-point in negotiating a settlement.

Summary

Tenant's break options are often made conditional upon the tenant having complied with its repairing obligations. The courts apply a strict standard of compliance, so that what may appear to be very minor matters can defeat the exercise of the break. Tenants are better placed if the condition requires only substantial, material or reasonable compliance with covenants.

In any event, the recommended course for tenants must be to have the property surveyed, and carry out any work revealed to be required.

Leaving chattels or tenant's fixtures such as demountable partitioning in the premises, as well as perhaps being a breach of a condition to comply with obligations to reinstate alterations, may well also be a breach of a condition to give vacant possession on the break date.

CHAPTER SIX

DILAPIDATIONS AT LEASE EXPIRY (1) – DAMAGES AT COMMON LAW

Content

This chapter deals with damages for breach of repairing obligation when the claim is made at expiry of the lease term. It considers the quantification of loss at common law.

Availability of remedies

Once a lease has terminated, specific performance of repair obligations becomes an impossibility. Forfeiture of the lease is likewise inapplicable, since what has ceased to exist cannot be forfeited. The Jervis v Harris procedure is unnecessary at that point, since termination of the lease means there is no impediment to the landlord entering the premises to carry out repairs.

What remains, as regards the enforcement of the repair obligation, is a claim for damages, the so-called 'terminal dilapidations claim'. It is also the case, of course, that sufficiently serious breach of the tenant's repairing obligation may be a ground for the landlord to oppose renewal of the lease, under *s.30(1)(a), Landlord and Tenant Act 1954*. This is not a means of enforcing the obligation, strictly speaking, and so falls outside the scope of this book.

Limitation of claims

At lease expiry, as indicated in Chapter 1, the landlord will be able to rely upon both of the usual parts of the repair covenant: the covenant to keep in repair throughout the term, and the covenant to yield up the premises in good repair at the end of the term. As regards the latter, performance is due at the moment of lease expiry; and as regards the former, all breaches of the covenant 'crystallise' at that time, so that on either basis the limitation period for the claim will run from that moment.

Unless the lease is one which fell within *s.54(2), Law of Property Act 1925* (a term of three years or less, taking effect as an interest in possession, at the full market rent), it will have been made in the form of a deed. The limitation period for bringing a claim, in that case, is twelve years from the end of the lease (*s.8, Limitation Act 1980*). Where the lease was not made by way of deed, the limitation period will be six years from the end of the lease (*s.5, Limitation Act 1980*).

Common law measure of damages

At common law the measure of damages for a tenant's failure to repair is the cost of the required repair work, plus loss of rent from the property during the time required to carry out the works (*Joyner v Weeks [1891] 2 QB 31*).

The recoverable damages are, however, capped by *s.18(1), Landlord and Tenant Act 1927*, so that the landlord cannot recover any more than the amount by which the value of its reversionary interest has been diminished as a consequence of the breach of repairing obligation. It is important to bear in mind that it is a cap, and that the measure of damages has not been changed by *s.18(1)*. To assess the quantum of a claim, it is therefore necessary first of all to calculate the amount of damages at common law, and then to determine by how much, if at all, the recoverable amount is limited by the operation of *s.18(1)*.

It should be noted that the cap applies only to repair covenants. Damages for breach of covenants to decorate, or to reinstate alterations, for example, are not capped. In the case of decoration, however, the distinction may be more apparent than real, since failure to decorate is often also a failure to repair, and *s.18(1)* has been applied so as to limit damages in such an event (*Latimer v Carney [2006] 3 EGLR 13*).

The reason for enacting *s.18(1)* was that the caselaw in relation to damages for breach of repairing covenant had developed in an anomalous way. It may be recalled from Chapter 3 that in a mid-term dilapidations claim, the common law measure of damages is the diminution in value of the landlord's interest (*Doe d. Worcester School Trustees v Rowlands (1841) 9 C & P 734*). At lease expiry, though, as described by Rigby LJ in *Ebbetts v Conquest [1895] 2 Ch 377*:

> *"...an arbitrary rule is laid down upon grounds of convenience, that whether or not the lessor in fact loses by the want of repair, he shall be paid the amount which would be necessary to place the premises in good repair."*

In *Joyner v Weeks* itself, Lord Esher MR justified the rule in this way:

> *"It is a highly convenient rule. It avoids* [here he is referring to arguments as to diminution in value of the landlord's interest] *all the subtle refinements with which we have been indulged today, and the extensive and costly inquiries which they would involve. It appears to me to be a simple and business-like rule..."*

Another justification was added by Wills J in *Henderson v Thorn [1893] 2 QB 164*:

> *"...but for this rule of law, a tenant who has broken his contract might come off better than if he had kept it; a result not to be lightly encouraged."*

The upshot was that in *Joyner v Weeks*, the landlord received the full cost of repairs even though a subsequent tenant had by then carried out work, some of which had remedied elements of the disrepair, and some of which had rendered other elements of the claimed repair work redundant. In *Inderwick v Leech (1885) 1 TLR 484*, and in *Rawlings v Morgan (1865) 18 CB (NS) 776*, the cost of repairs was awarded in damages even though the premises had been demolished.

This approach was clearly a departure from the basic principle that the function of an award of damages is to compensate the claimant for his loss. The effect of *s.18(1)* can therefore be seen as wrenching the law of dilapidations back into alignment with the general common law of damages, and there are suggestions to that effect in the judgment of HH Judge Toulmin QC in *PGF II SA v Royal & Sun Alliance Insurance Plc [2011] 1 P&CR 11*. The fact that the law in Scotland (where *s.18(1)* does not apply), developing independently of that of England and Wales, has arrived at a broadly similar way of assessing damages for disrepair, gives some support to that view.

Even since the enactment of *s.18(1)*, mitigating the effect of the *Joyner v Weeks* rule, there have been attempts to challenge that rule. An argument that there was no such rule was advanced in *Shortlands Investments v Cargill [1995] 1 EGLR 51* (though rejected by the court), and it was suggested in the judgment in *Latimer v Carney [2006] 3 EGLR 13*, as well as in the *PGF II SA* case, that a different common law measure might be adopted in appropriate cases. However, the conventional approach has more recently been endorsed in *Sunlife Europe Properties v Tiger Aspect Holdings [2013] EWHC 463 (TCC)*, and also in *Hammersmatch Properties v Saint-Gobain Ceramics & Plastics [2013] EWHC 1161*.

The general understanding remains, accordingly, that at common law the *Joyner v Weeks* measure applies, but that it may be capped by the operation of *s.18(1)*. Despite the disparagement of Lord Esher in *Joyner v Weeks*, therefore, "*subtle refinements*" and "*extensive and costly inquiries*" form an unavoidable part of the process of assessing damages for breach of repairing covenant at lease expiry.

The first part of the process, though, consists of the common law *Joyner v Weeks* exercise of determining the cost of the repairs, and any loss of rent.

Cost of repairs

Where the landlord has not carried out the repair work, determining this element of the damages is a matter of identifying (a) what work by the tenant would amount to compliance with the repair covenant, applying the principles of interpretation discussed in Chapter 1, and (b) what its reasonable cost would be (including any professional fees which would reasonably be incurred).

In the event that the landlord has done the work, then the inquiry is rather simpler, since actual cost figures will be available. However, it may still be relevant to consider whether the work carried out has gone beyond work of repair in any respect, and to exclude the costs of any such 'extra' work from the assessment of damages.

There may also be a question as to which method of repair should form the basis of the assessment. To revisit an example given in Chapter 1: an external wall may require re-rendering; it could be done with a relatively inexpensive traditional sand and cement render, or a superior polymer or spraystone render. Either would be a reasonable method of remedying the disrepair, but there is a cost difference. The tenant would presumably carry out the work at the least expense, and that is the basis on which the court would assess the damages (e.g. *Ultraworth Ltd v General Accident Fire & Life Assurance [2000] 2 EGLR 115*). This principle applies whether or not the landlord has actually carried out the work by the more expensive method; the recoverable damages will still be assessed by reference to the cheaper method.

Situations may arise in which it is impracticable to remedy the disrepair on a like-for-like basis. In a service charge case, *Craighead v Homes for Islington [2010] UKUT 47 (LC)*, the Lands Chamber of the Upper Tribunal held that the replacement of single-glazed windows with double-glazed windows fell within the recoverable costs of 'repair'. Building regulations require the use of double-glazing, and it may be virtually impossible to buy new single-glazed units.

Or to take a hypothetical example, the tenant may be responsible for repair of the air-conditioning system within a building, which at the end of the lease is 25 years old, and has come to the end of its service life. It will simply not be possible to find a new replacement of exactly the same specification as the old system. Technology has moved on, different refrigerants are used, environmental and efficiency requirements are more demanding, and the new system will therefore almost inevitably represent an improvement to some extent. That should not, however, enable the tenant to obtain any discount for 'betterment' (*Harbutt's "Plasticene" Ltd v Wayne Tank & Pump Co [1970] 1 QB 447*).

On the other hand, a 25-year-old system was probably not designed to cope with the amount of heat generated within the building by extensive computer use, and the landlord may choose to replace the old system with one which can handle the increased load. That would be work going beyond repair, and a discount from the cost of replacement should apply in determining the amount of damages (*Sunlife Europe Properties v Tiger Aspect Holdings [2013] EWHC 463 (TCC)*).

Relevance of tax issues

The impact of Value Added Tax should also be mentioned. Depending upon the landlord's tax position, it may or may not be able to recover any VAT incurred on the repair work. If it can recover the VAT, or if it has no intention of carrying out the repair work, then VAT should not be included in the amount of recoverable damages. If, however, it cannot recover the VAT, and has done the work or intends to do so, then VAT should be included (*Drummond v S & U Stores Ltd [1981] 1 EGLR 42*).

That is perhaps little more than an instance of the obligation which falls upon any litigant claiming damages to mitigate their loss. If the landlord is entitled to recover VAT incurred on repair work but fails to do so, then it will have failed to mitigate its loss, and the recoverable damages will be reduced by the amount it would have recovered. In the same way, it has been suggested (though this has not yet featured in any reported case) that where a landlord is in a position to claim capital allowances through incurring expenditure on the repairs, the amount of damages they may recover should be reduced by the amount they are entitled to claim.

HM Revenue & Customs have recently resolved one uncertainty (of their own making), over whether a payment by a tenant to a landlord for dilapidations should itself be subject to VAT. The conventional understanding is that a payment of damages for breach of contract is not a payment for a supply of goods or services, and hence not subject to VAT. However, prompted by two cases (concerning early termination payments under consumer contracts) decided in the Court of Justice of the European Union, HMRC published *Revenue and Customs Brief 12 (2020)*, announcing a change in policy.

The essence of the matter was that dilapidations payments could be considered as an extra payment for use of the premises. If the tenant were not under an obligation to return the premises in repair, then it would likely pay a higher rent to reflect that. Landlords and tenants might therefore agree a lower rate of rent, thus reducing VAT liability, on the basis that there would be a compensatory dilapidations payment. Such payments should therefore be subject to VAT, provided that the landlord had opted to tax the property.

Following strong adverse reaction, and pending further guidance, HMRC announced that businesses could either treat dilapidations payments as subject to VAT or not. Revised guidance subsequently emerged in the form of *Revenue and Customs Brief 2 (2022)*, stating that dilapidations payments will normally remain outside the scope of VAT (although HMRC has indicated that it may depart from this policy if it finds evidence of value shifting from rent to dilapidations payments to avoid accounting for VAT).

Professional fees and exploratory investigations

Carrying out the work will often involve incurring professional fees, in preparing plans and drawings, drawing up a specification of works, receiving and assessing tenders, appointment of contractors and supervision of the work. If reasonably and properly incurred, the amount of those fees, plus VAT if applicable, should be included in the calculation of damages.

One issue often encountered in relation to fees concerns the cost of inspections and exploratory work. Where a schedule of dilapidations purports to require the tenant, for example, to have the electrical installation tested, or the drains surveyed, that is generally something which the tenant can safely ignore, unless there is some specific provision in the lease requiring that such investigations be carried out by the tenant. It is for the landlord to determine whether there is any disrepair, and then to pursue its remedies against the tenant.

For the same reason, professional fees in relation to investigative work should generally not be included in the damages claim (*Commercial Union v Label Ink [2001] L&TR 29*). However, if a specific defect is known about, but investigative work is needed to identify the precise extent of the defect and the appropriate work required to put it right, then it may be permissible to include fees incurred in those investigations (*Plough Investments v Manchester City Council [1989] 1 EGLR 244*).

Loss of rent

It is a convenient and conventional shorthand to refer to the 'loss of rent' element of the claim, although it is potentially rather misleading. The justification for including loss of rent in the calculation of damages is essentially that the property cannot be marketed until the repairs have been done. Had the property been returned to the landlord in good repair, it would have been marketed immediately, and it might be anticipated that rental flow would resume after a period of, say, three months. The need to spend, say, two months carrying out repairs before it can be marketed, means that the three-month marketing period does not begin at the end of the term, but at the end of the two-month repair period, hence the total rental void is five months. The landlord has lost rent for a period equating to the two months required for carrying out the repair work.

The reason why the expression 'loss of rent' is misleading is that this head of damages extends to matters other than rent. The landlord can take into account all heads of lost income, and outgoings incurred, during the period: service charge, insurance premiums, and business rates, for example, and also rent payable to any superior landlord. It might be more accurate to refer to 'property cost'; however, the implications of 'loss of rent' are well understood.

While loss of rent is conventionally a part of the calculation of damages, it must be shown that the landlord has actually suffered loss in this respect. The tenant might argue that the market is so slack that any work could comfortably be carried out during the likely duration of any letting period (e.g. *Firle Investments v Datapoint International [2000] EWHC 105*). Another possible challenge is that the landlord intends to carry out refurbishment works, in addition to the repair works, which would prevent letting the premises for at least as long as the period required to do the repairs.

By way of illustration, the loss of rent element featured in *Consortium Commercial Developments Ltd v ABB Ltd [2015] EWHC 2128 (TCC)*. In that case, the lease had expired in June 2011. Despite the passage of time between then and the trial date in 2015, the tenant's breaches of covenant at the property had still not been remedied by the landlord.

The landlord's position was that it wished to recover damages from the tenant before spending money on the repairs. It also considered that it would be more sensible to wait for the market to improve in order to achieve a better rent, rather than carrying out expensive works and offering the premises prematurely at a comparatively low rent.

It was agreed that the works would take around 12 weeks to complete. The landlord's claim included loss of rent and rates during that period, amounting to £45,666. It was common ground between the parties that, given the weak state of the market in 2011, the property had little prospect of being let while out of repair.

The judge concluded that the property would not have let promptly even if it had been in good condition, and rejected this element of the claim:

> "*As regards the contention that the whole marketing process was delayed, a difficulty which the claimant faces is that it is artificial to regard the marketing period as a set period of time such that, if commencement is delayed, the achievement of a transaction will be correspondingly delayed. In poor market conditions it might take a year or even several years to find a suitable and willing tenant. When such a tenant is found, it will probably make no difference to the timing of the transaction with that tenant whether the property has been on the market for, say, 18 months prior to that tenant's introduction or for, say, 15 months prior to that event.*"

Summary

A claim for damages is the only applicable remedy at lease expiry.

The common law measure of damages consists of two elements: the cost of the relevant repairs, and the loss of income from the property during the period required to carry out the repairs. (The recoverable amount is, however, restricted by *s.18(1), Landlord and Tenant Act 1927*, covered in the next chapter).

In a case where the landlord has not carried out the repairs, cost of repair must be assessed by reference to the work which the tenant could properly have been required to do.

In a case where the landlord has done the repairs, the actual cost is the starting-point, though it may be reduced to reflect any element of improvement going beyond repair, and the availability of cheaper methods of doing the work. Where the landlord cannot recover the input VAT on the cost of the repairs, and either has done the work or intends to do so, then the VAT element should be included in the damages award.

Professional fees reasonably incurred in supervision of the work, etc., are generally recoverable.

Costs relating to investigative and exploratory works (e.g. electrical surveys) may be recoverable if incurred to identify the extent of a known issue, and the appropriate method of addressing it.

Loss of income from the property during the period required to carry out the repairs, and outgoings on the property during that period, are in principle recoverable, though the landlord must establish that it has actually suffered loss in this respect.

CHAPTER SEVEN

DILAPIDATIONS AT LEASE EXPIRY (2) – IMPACT OF S.18(1) AND PREPARATION FOR LEASE EXPIRY

Content

This chapter considers *s.18(1), Landlord and Tenant Act 1927*, which restricts the recoverable amount of damages in a claim for breach of repairing covenant. It also covers the assessment of damages for breach of other covenants which bear on the physical condition of the property, such as a failure to reinstate. Finally, it addresses issues which may arise in preparing for lease expiry, to increase the chances of a good outcome on the issue of dilapidations.

s.18(1), Landlord and Tenant Act 1927

As previously outlined, this provision limits the amount of recoverable damages. It has what are usually referred to as two 'limbs'.

The first limb

> *"Damages for a breach of a covenant or agreement to keep or put premises in repair during the currency of a lease, or to leave or put premises in repair at the termination of the lease, whether such covenant or agreement is expressed or implied, and whether general or specific, shall in no case exceed the amount (if any) by which the value of the reversion (whether immediate or not) in the premises is diminished owing to the breach of such covenant or agreement as aforesaid..."*

The second limb

"...and in particular no damage shall be recovered for a breach of any such covenant or agreement to leave or put premises in repair at the termination of a lease, if it is shown that the premises, in whatever state of repair they might be, would at or shortly after the termination of the tenancy have been or be pulled down, or such structural alterations made therein as would render valueless the repairs covered by the covenant or agreement"

It will be noticed that both limbs are applicable at lease expiry, while it is only the first limb which applies in mid-term. The jargon in common use is to refer to the issue raised by the first limb as 'diminution', and that raised by the second limb as 'supersession' (the landlord's works would 'supersede' any repairs which the tenant should otherwise be responsible for).

Diminution in value

In relation to the first limb, it is necessary to identify the diminution in value of the landlord's reversion as a result of the breaches of repairing covenant.

Where the landlord has actually carried out the repair work, or clearly intends to do so, the cost of the work will *prima facie* represent the diminution in value of the reversion, and so a landlord in that position will not need to adduce any valuation evidence (*Jones v Herxheimer [1950] 2 KB 106; Smiley v Townshend [1950] 2 KB 311*). This applies also where an incoming tenant has carried out the work at the landlord's expense (whether through a rent-free period, or the landlord actually funding the work). If, in such a case, the tenant contends that there is no diminution in value, the burden of proving that is on the tenant (*Mather v Barclays Bank [1987] 2 EGLR 254*). In a particular instance it may have been unreasonable for the landlord to carry out the works, and in that case the cost should not be taken as a guide to the diminution in value.

Where the landlord has not carried out the repair work, it will be necessary for the parties to have 's.18 valuations' or 'diminution valuations' carried out. In these circumstances the burden of proving diminution in value is on the landlord.

Carrying out s.18 valuations is a specialised business, and there are surprisingly few valuers who are really familiar with this area of practice. The exercise involves (a) a valuation of the building on the hypothesis that it is in a condition consistent with the tenant having complied with its repairing covenants, and (b) another valuation, in the actual state of disrepair in which the tenant has left it. Then (b) is deducted from (a), and the resulting figure is the *s.18(1)* cap. For the purpose of both valuations, the value is determined as at the date of expiry of the lease.

In practice the cap may often be little different from the cost of works and loss of rent, as the method of valuing the building in disrepair may be (over-simplifying somewhat) to deduct, from the figure which would have been paid for it in repair, the expense that a buyer would incur in putting it into repair. *Shortlands Investments Ltd v Cargill plc [1995] 1 EGLR 51* provides a good instance of this sort of s.18 valuation. This approach is often adopted, and may well be a good reflection of the likely approach of a buyer in negotiating the purchase price. However, it may be criticised in that it assumes what it seeks to prove: by treating the cost of the works as the basis for calculating the diminution in the value of the reversion, it takes for granted that the disrepair has given rise to a diminution in value. However, the valuer can only proceed on this basis if he has made the judgement that the buyer would consider it worthwhile to carry out the repairs, which will not always be the case.

What might a s.18 valuation look like?

The valuation approach used in *Shortlands v Cargill* is not the only one possible, but because it is often adopted it merits closer attention. The logic behind the approach is as follows.

The valuation exercise is one of ascertaining what the property might have sold for in a hypothetical transaction at the expiry of the term. In fact, there are two hypothetical sales: one of the property in its actual state of disrepair at lease expiry, and the other of the property in an assumed condition representing compliance by the tenant with its repair obligations. Other than the state of repair, the two properties are identical, and the valuation date is the same

There will be a period of time, in relation to each hypothetical transaction, before the property can be re-let. The hypothetical purchaser will naturally do whatever is going to secure the best return on his investment, and that may mean carrying out some refurbishment work before re-letting. That applies to both hypothetical sales; however, the need to carry out repair work applies to only one of them. But once the works have been carried out to each property (refurbishment in one case, refurbishment plus repair in the other) they will have the same end value.

The enquiry is therefore what is the financial impact in each case of achieving the end value, starting from the valuation date.

In *Shortlands v Cargill*, the outcome of that analysis was appended to the judgment, and it is helpful to consider it here.

A. Valuation assuming Tenant's compliance with covenants

A.1 Estimated value let and in good repair			
	36,888ft² @ £23.50	£866,868	
Less headrent	36,888ft² @ £17.62	£649,967	
	Profit rent:		£216,901
89 years' purchase at 17% – sinking fund attracting 4% and 35% tax thereon			x5.82
Estimated value let and in good repair			£1,262,364

A.2 Deductions:			
Deficit of headrent for 30 weeks		£374,981	
Non-recoverable service charge for 30 weeks		£148,390	
Void rates		£55,626	
Interest on rent, service charge and rates		£27,079	
Letting fees (15% plus VAT)		£152,785	
Marketing costs		£50,000	
Profit to purchaser @ 25% of gross value		£315,591	
Works			
(a) cost	£165,648		
(b) fees and VAT	£48,452		
(c) interest	£12,846		
Total cost of work		£226,946	
Acquisition costs		£10,000	
Total deductions unrelated to purchase price			£1,361,398
			-£99,034
Interest for 30 weeks on reverse premium (credit)			-£6,412
A.3 Net value: Estimated value unlet and in state of repair envisaged by tenant's covenants			**-£92,622**

B. Valuation in actual state of repair and decoration

B.1 Estimated value let and in good repair			
	36,888ft^2 @ £23.50	£866,868	
Less headrent	36,888ft^2 @ £17.62	£649,967	
	Profit rent:		£216,901
89 years' purchase at 17% – sinking fund attracting 4% and 35% tax thereon			x5.82
Estimated value let and in good repair			£1,262,364
B.2 Deductions:			
Deficit of headrent for 41 weeks		£512,474	
Non-recoverable service charge for 41 weeks		£202,800	
Void rates		£83,805	
Interest on rent, service charge and rates		£48,033	
Letting fees (15% plus VAT)		£152,785	
Marketing costs		£50,000	
Profit to purchaser @ 25% of gross value		£315,591	
Works			
(a) cost	£235,464		
(b) fees and VAT	£68,873		
(c) interest	£18,260		

Total cost of work	£322,597	
Acquisition costs	£10,000	
Total deductions unrelated to purchase price		<u>£1,698,085</u>
			-£435,721
Interest for 41 weeks on reverse premium (credit)		-£38,500
B.3 Net value: Estimated value unlet and in actual state of disrepair		-£397,221

It can be seen, comparing the two valuations, that the difference is largely accounted for by a higher cost of works and loss of rent (41 weeks as opposed to 30 weeks) in the second valuation. That reflects a calculation on a 'refurbishment plus repair' basis, as compared to the 'refurbishment only' basis of the first valuation. Other differences are consequential: fees calculated on a percentage of the cost of works, and interest calculated on certain items.

The difference between the two valuations (i.e. the *s.18(1)* cap) exceeded the cost of works and loss of rent. The landlord was therefore able to recover damages on the full common law basis.

Of course, the figures in the valuations would change depending on the court's conclusions as to cost of repair, and time required to carry out the repairs. A valuation of this nature may therefore need to be prepared on alternative bases, in anticipation of a range of outcomes on the other issues in the case as to what repair the tenant is properly responsible for, and its cost.

One noteworthy feature of the case is that the market conditions were such that even in repair, the property had a negative value: the landlord would have had to pay someone to take it off their hands. That did not prevent calculation of the diminution in value of the reversion, although the tenant argued that once the value had dropped to nil, it could not diminish further. The court upheld the landlord's argument that if the out-of-repair valuation was even more negative, so that the landlord would have to pay a buyer even more to take the property, then that difference represented the diminution in value.

Other approaches to diminution in value

It might appear that on the basis of that sort of approach, *s.18(1)* would never have the effect of restricting the amount of damages recoverable. However, the circumstances may engage *s.18(1)* in different ways, and there is no shortage of reported cases in which it has operated so as to reduce the damages award, such as *Jaquin v Holland [1960] 1 WLR 258* and *Shane v Runwell [1967] EGD 88*.

For example, if the evidence indicates that the demand for the particular type of property is sufficiently strong that it will be possible for the landlord to let it at a full rent (or sell its interest at a full price) without undertaking any works, conceding a schedule of condition, or making any financial allowance for the disrepair, then it will be very difficult for the landlord to demonstrate any diminution, and recover any damages.

Again, the evidence may indicate that what has been a commercial property has no longer any worthwhile value as such, and that any hypothetical purchaser of the property would either demolish it and redevelop the site, or perhaps convert the building to another use (a scenario now encountered fairly frequently, with the planning policy climate currently favouring re-purposing). In such a situation, the diminution in value as a result of any disrepair may well be nil (e.g. *Ultraworth v General Accident Fire & Life Assurance [2000] 2 EGLR 115*).

That sort of consideration may also apply to reduce, rather than completely eliminate, the diminution in value, where the evidence is that any hypothetical purchaser would carry out significant upgrading works, which would make much of the disrepair irrelevant. In such a case, diminution would be assessed only by reference to the items of disrepair unaffected by the probable upgrading works (*Firle Investments v Datapoint International [2000] EWHC 105*).

Another factor might be the existence of sub-leases on the valuation date.

- If the dilapidations claim arises upon surrender of the headlease, then any sub-leases will survive, and will be directly enforceable by the landlord.

- If on the other hand the headlease has expired by effluxion of time, then any sub-leases must also have expired; or if the headlease has been terminated by exercise of a break option, then sub-leases granted out of it will have been terminated too (*Pennell v Payne [1995] QB 192*). Nevertheless, in either case, if the sub-tenancies were within the *Landlord and Tenant Act 1954*, then they may be continuing under *s.24* of that Act beyond the expiry date, and there may be every expectation that the sub-tenants will exercise their right to renew on the same terms as under the old sub-leases.

- In those situations, the landlord may not be at any disadvantage as a result of the disrepair. It will take the benefit of the repair obligations undertaken by the sub-tenants, and will be entitled to receive the rent without having to make any concessions to reflect the disrepair.

- There is a doubt as to whether the rent upon renewal would be discounted to reflect the disrepair, as discussed in Chapter 3, but the balance of authority to date suggests not. In *Family Management v Gray [1980] 1 EGLR 46*, the presence at the property of sub-tenants holding over under the 1954 Act, with full repairing obligations and every intention to renew, led the court to conclude that there was no diminution in value of the reversion as a result of the disrepair.

Supersession

The impact of the second limb of *s.18(1)* is often referred to as 'supersession'. This refers to the position where repairs would otherwise be necessary at lease termination, but the landlord intends to demolish the property or carry out structural alterations upon it, which would make the repairs valueless. The landlord's intended works are said to 'supersede' the repairs, and no damages are recoverable.

It may be noted that the second limb begins with the words "and in particular", which suggests that it is merely a specific instance of the first limb. This need not necessarily be the case. In *Marquess of Salisbury v Gilmore [1942] 2 KB 38*, a lease term expired a matter of weeks after the start of the Second World War. The landlord had decided to demolish and redevelop the property some two years beforehand, and had informed his tenant of that. However, three days before lease expiry, he was advised by his agents not to contemplate a new building while there was a risk of war damage, and so decided not to demolish and redevelop after all. The case turned on factual questions of when the change of mind came, before or after the end of the term, and when it was communicated to the tenant. In the end it was held that the second limb applied: at the end of the term the landlord did still intend to demolish and redevelop. The landlord therefore failed, but it does not follow that there was not substantial and provable diminution in the value of the reversion.

It should be noted that the second limb focuses only upon demolition and structural alterations. It is easy to imagine other types of work which the landlord might have decided to carry out which would equally render valueless any repairs, but which would not engage the second limb.

That consideration leads to some debate about whether there is a common law doctrine of supersession quite apart from *s.18(1)*. Say that a 25-year old office building is equipped with the original air-conditioning equipment, which is on its last legs. The landlord plans to replace the air-conditioning with new plant, which will be of a much higher specification. That new plant would supersede the necessity of repairing the old plant, although the work would not be demolition or structural work so as to engage *s.18(1)*. Nevertheless, it would clearly affect the recoverable damages, the landlord being able to recover only the notional cost of like-for-like repair (*Sunlife Europe Properties v Tiger Aspect Holdings [2013] 2 P&CR 4*). This tends to support the view that the effect of *s.18(1)* was to re-align the assessment of damages in disrepair cases with the conventional common law approach, focusing on the loss actually suffered by the claimant.

It is conventional to address the second limb in terms of the intentions of the actual landlord, although the wording of the section does not support that interpretation. Might it apply, regardless of the actual landlord's intention, in circumstances where any reasonable landlord would pull down the building and redevelop the site? So far no reported case has approached it on that basis, and the investigation is always into the state of mind of the actual landlord.

For the second limb of *s.18(1)* to apply, the landlord's intention must be sufficiently firm: *Cunliffe v Goodman [1950] 2 KB 237*. The classic quotation from that case says that the landlord's intention must have *"moved out of the zone of contemplation – out of the sphere of the tentative, the provisional and the exploratory – into the valley of decision"*.

PGF II SA v Royal & Sun Alliance Insurance Plc [2011] 1 P&CR 11 illustrated that if the landlord can demonstrate that its intention was genuinely unformed at lease expiry, then carrying out an extensive refurbishment later will not bar the recovery of substantial damages under *s.18(1)*. A careful landlord, therefore, might ensure that the 'paper trail' makes it plain that there has been no decision prior to the contractual term date, in relation to carrying out relevant work. Instead, the evidence must show that the landlord is keeping its options open; it might be a good idea to put off any planning application until after lease expiry, for example.

Landlord's intentions and timing of claim

The above account of the two limbs of *s.18(1)* explains an observation made in discussing damages claims in mid-term, in Chapter 3. It is apparent that factors to do with the likely immediate future of the property, and the landlord's intentions in relation to the property, are highly relevant. Whether any sub-tenants intend to renew their leases; whether redevelopment appears a good option; whether upgrading is needed; whether an incoming tenant would pay less because of any disrepair; or whether the landlord might need to concede a schedule of condition, or pay for repairs itself, are all factors which will affect the assessment of damages, and also the landlord's actions. These factors might be no less relevant when bringing a damages claim in mid-term; however, information as to those matters may at that time be unavailable or sketchy at best. At the end of the term, the information is all there.

Along with the impact of the *Leasehold Property (Repairs) Act 1938*, this factor tends to push dilapidations claim to the end of the lease, and to discourage claims mid-term.

Damages for failure to reinstate, decorate, etc

In the case of breaches of covenant relating to the physical condition of the property, other than the repair covenant, the damages are to be assessed on normal principles by ascertaining what loss the landlord has actually suffered. In *James v Hutton [1950] 1 KB 9*, the tenant of a shop installed a new shop-front, pursuant to a licence to alter. The licence contained an obligation to reinstate if required to do so by the landlord at the end of the lease. The landlord notified the tenant that it was so required, but the tenant failed to reinstate. The landlord claimed the cost of reinstatement as damages, but it was held that no loss had been suffered. The landlord had not done the work, and there was no evidence of intention to carry out the work, nor any evidence that the altered shop-front was inappropriate or affected the lettability of the premises in any way.

The general view, accordingly, is that in cases where the landlord has not reinstated and does not intend to do so, the court is likely to look first at whether the value of the landlord's interest has been reduced by the failure to reinstate. The assessment is essentially the same as that carried out under the first limb of *s.18(1)* (which further supports the suggestion that the effect of that section was to bring the law on damages for breach of repairing covenant back into alignment with general common law principles).

If the landlord has reinstated, or intends to do so, then the damages are likely to equate to the cost of the works, plus loss of income during the period required to carry them out, in the same way as for breach of a repair obligation. Potentially no damages would be recoverable if there were circumstances making it unreasonable for the landlord to carry out the reinstatement; the court might also look particularly closely at the genuineness of a stated intention to reinstate, if the alterations had actually increased the value of the landlord's interest.

It has been mentioned earlier that *s.18(1)* has been held to apply to damages for failure to decorate, where the lack of decoration amounted to disrepair (*Latimer v Carney [2006] 3 EGLR 13*). It is therefore only in cases of 'pure' failure to decorate, falling short of disrepair, that the principles just discussed would apply.

Preparation for lease expiry

Tenant undertaking repair

Bearing in mind the implications of *s.18(1)*, it is often advisable for the tenant to carry out repairs to the property itself in advance of lease expiry, even if no schedule has yet been served. The advantages are:

- The tenant retains control of the extent and cost of the works.

- The landlord's ability to claim for loss of rent will be severely restricted.

- The landlord may find it much more difficult to establish diminution in the value of the reversion when a significant element of the disrepair has been remedied, particularly since the tenant can choose what work to do on the basis of whether it will really make a difference to value.

There are some disadvantages, though:

- Any ability to rely on a supersession argument will be lost.

- A potential advantage as regards VAT recovery may be lost. This is a slightly rarefied point, and depends upon consideration of the VAT position of both landlord and tenant: it has been discussed previously that where the landlord would recover the VAT element of the cost of any repair work, that cannot form part of a damages claim. Not all tenants achieve full VAT recovery (financial services institutions, for example, recover a low proportion of input VAT), so if a tenant in that position leaves repair work to be done by the landlord, which *will* recover the VAT, the cost saving is 16.6%.

Another factor in making this judgement is what the landlord is really trying to achieve. A landlord with plans to reconfigure or refurbish a property may actually find it inconvenient to have the property returned to them repaired, in its existing format. It may be much more attractive to them to have a financial settlement from the tenant, which will partly fund the work they have in mind, whether it is work of repair or not. In that case, a tenant who indicates an intention to carry out repair work may find itself in a position to negotiate a favourable settlement with the landlord. Timing remains important, though: it is not unknown (particularly in cases of conditional break clauses) for a tenant to begin a programme of works, but ultimately run out of time to complete it, due to lack of planning and preparation.

Key date management

Making sure that applicable deadlines are not missed is a particular issue for landlords, but may also be important for a tenant who intends to pass any liability down to a sub-tenant. It will be rare (though not unknown) for a landlord to miss the limitation period for bringing a dilapidations claim – usually 12 years after lease expiry, as discussed earlier. However, there are other dates which are equally important but less obvious:

- Where the landlord's intended works on the property include, not just repairs, but also work that will affect common parts or the structure, the landlord will look to recover its expenditure on those areas via the service charge. As a matter of construction of the lease, it may be necessary for the work to have been completed, and the service charge contribution computed and demanded, prior to lease expiry. In the case of mixed-use premises, the residential regime under the *Landlord and Tenant Act 1985* may apply, and *s.20B* requires that all expenditure be demanded within 18 months of being incurred, or it becomes irrecoverable.

- If the landlord wishes the tenant to reinstate any alterations, the terms of the lease or licence may stipulate that the tenant is obliged to reinstate only if required to do so by the landlord. Usually, the landlord has until the end of the term to raise that requirement, but some leases provide for a deadline at some time before lease expiry.

- The lease may entitle the landlord to recover its costs of preparing and serving a schedule of dilapidations, but if the schedule is only served after the end of the lease, or perhaps if the costs are only demanded after the end of the lease, they may be irrecoverable. This is a matter of interpretation of the lease.

- If the landlord has used the Jervis v Harris procedure in the run-up to lease expiry, doing repair work itself and recovering the cost from the tenant, the work must have been completed and the demand sent to the tenant before the expiry of the lease.

- Tenants may seek to use a counterclaim for compensation for improvements under *s.1, Landlord and Tenant Act 1927*, to negotiate down the landlord's claim (this is considered further in the next chapter). The time limits for doing so are contained in *s.47, Landlord and Tenant Act 1954*, and depend on how the termination of the tenancy has come about. The deadline may in some circumstances (including simple effluxion of time) be prior to the termination of the lease, so care is needed with this.

Documents

The scheme of the *Civil Procedure Rules* is designed to ensure early identification and exchange of information. Nevertheless, documents do turn up late, perhaps because their relevance or importance has been overlooked, for example a deed of variation or licence to alter which should have been taken into account in preparing the schedule of dilapidations. Care should be taken to identify and assemble all relevant documents early.

Tenants often fail to record the condition of the premises when they vacate, yet this is potentially vital information for challenging items in the schedule of dilapidations. It may also be valuable in circumstances where damage is caused to the premises after the end of the lease, for example by vandals or squatters, and there is a need to establish what damage was existing at lease expiry and what came later.

Clients also need to be careful about maintaining privilege in relation to documents such as early advice on condition or valuation, which they may wish to avoid disclosing in any subsequent proceedings. They should also be mindful of generating documents in other contexts which will be unhelpful as regards any proceedings, such as a tenant's filed accounts which contain provision for the landlord's dilapidations claim.

Summary

The recoverable amount of damages in a terminal dilapidations claim is restricted by *s.18(1), Landlord and Tenant Act 1927*, so that the landlord can recover no more than the amount by which the value of its interest in the property is diminished in consequence of the disrepair. Further, if there will be, at or shortly after the end of the lease, demolition or structural works which would render repairs valueless, then the landlord may not recover any damages at all in relation to those repairs (this principle is commonly referred to as 'supersession').

As regards diminution in value, where the landlord has carried out repair work, then the cost of repair will prima facie be regarded as indicating the amount of the diminution. If the landlord has not carried out repairs, valuation evidence will be needed.

As regards supersession, the scope of this principle is limited to works of demolition or structural alterations to be carried out by the landlord, although at common law other landlord's works may also have an impact on the amount of recoverable damages. The landlord's intention to carry out the relevant works must be one which is firm and settled, at the expiry of the lease, for this principle to apply.

Damages for breach of non-repairing covenants which relate to the physical condition of the property are assessed in a similar way to the approach taken under the first limb of *s.18(1)*: if the landlord has done the work, the cost will usually represent the amount of damages; if not, the court will assess the impact, if any, of the breach upon the value of the landlord's interest.

In preparing for lease expiry:

- Tenants should give consideration to doing some or all of the required repair work themselves. This has pros and cons, depending on the particular circumstances.

- There are a variety of key dates and deadlines for both parties to be aware of.

- Care should be taken in assembling and considering all relevant documentation, keeping a good record of the condition of the property at lease expiry, and preserving privilege in sensitive documents.

CHAPTER EIGHT

ISSUES RELATING TO TENANT'S ALTERATIONS

Content

This chapter addresses the consequences at lease expiry of alterations made to the property by the tenant during the term. It considers: the tenant's right to claim compensation for improvements; the classification of items as having become either part of the land, landlord's fixtures, tenant's fixtures or chattels; and the implications for the scope of repair obligations. Also covered are reinstatement obligations, and specific considerations in relation to partitions, carpets and ceiling tiles.

Licences to alter

Obligations in leases, or any other type of contract for that matter, generally fall to be interpreted against the factual matrix at the time the contract was entered into. That may mean that an obligation to repair 'the premises' is to be interpreted as meaning the premises as they stood at the time the lease was granted, and not as subsequently altered and added to.

It is always possible for the parties to provide otherwise, in the lease or in a licence to alter, and it is when consent is granted for alterations that landlord and tenant both need to be mindful about what they want to happen at the end of the lease. Should the alterations be reinstated at that time? In the meantime, should the repair obligations extend to the alterations? Are any items to be removable by the tenant at the end of the lease term? Many of the issues which arise in terminal dilapidations claims could be avoided if specific, clear provision were to be made for these matters when licences to alter come to be negotiated.

That said, problems sometimes arise because provision made in licences, in relation to the specific alterations, conflicts with the existing, general lease terms. It is all too common to find conflicts such as: a lease which provides that all alterations are to be reinstated at lease expiry, and that repair obligations do not extend to alterations; and a licence which applies all obligations of the lease to the alterations, and provides that reinstatement at lease expiry shall be at the landlord's option.

s.3, Landlord and Tenant Act 1927

There is a low level of awareness of the provisions of *s.3, Landlord and Tenant Act 1927*, which aims to confer rights upon a tenant who wishes to carry out alterations to a property, but whose landlord objects to the works. It is worth summarising *s.3* briefly at this point, because it may become relevant when a tenant is faced with a dilapidations claim at lease end.

A tenant who wants to carry out improvements can serve a notice on the landlord of its intention to do so (the section refers to 'improvements' rather than 'alterations', but as a consequence of *Lambert v F W Woolworth & Co [1938] Ch 883*, it is difficult to conceive of any alterations which would not be regarded as 'improvements' for this purpose). There is no prescribed form for the notice under *s.3*, but it must be accompanied by a plan and specification which shows the improvements and the part of the property affected by them, in sufficient detail to enable the landlord to reach a decision. Ideally the notice should also make it clear that the tenant is intending to exercise its rights under *s.3*, although a specific reference to the rights under the 1927 Act may not be necessary (*Deerfield Travel Services Limited v Leathersellers Company (1983) 46 P&CR 132*). It is likely that many, even most, letters requesting consent for alterations constitute *s.3* notices, without either the sender or the recipient knowing it.

If the landlord does not object to the improvements within three months of the notice, then the tenant may lawfully carry them out, even if the lease would prohibit this.

Instead of objecting to the works, a landlord can offer to do them itself in return for a reasonable increase in the rent (determined by the county court if not agreed). A tenant is under no obligation to accept this offer and may withdraw its notice. If it does so, the landlord then has no right to carry out the works and increase the rent – equally the tenant would not be entitled to carry out the works, and so an unsatisfactory stalemate would result.

If the landlord does object, then the tenant has the right to apply to the court for authorisation to carry out the improvements. The court can authorise the improvements if they:

- Are calculated to add to the letting value of the property at the termination of the tenancy

- Are reasonable and suitable to the character of the property

- Will not diminish the value of any other property which belongs to the landlord or to any superior landlord.

The court may modify the plans and specification of the works and impose conditions as it thinks fit.

After completing the works, the tenant should apply to the landlord for a certificate that the works have been duly executed. If the landlord fails to give this certificate within one month, or refuses to give it, then the certificate can be issued by the court instead, upon the tenant's application. If the tenant wants to claim compensation at the end of the term, this certificate is evidentially useful.

Compensation for improvements

It is the potential for claiming compensation at the end of the term that is relevant for present purposes. The right to compensation for improvements made pursuant to the s.3 procedure is set out in s.1 of the 1927 Act. Contracting-out is not possible. The person entitled to the compensation is the tenant in possession, whether the improvements were carried out by them or by a predecessor in title. A tenant who has sublet the whole, and is therefore not in possession, is not entitled to claim compensation. The position of a tenant who has sublet part is not clear.

The entitlement to compensation arises at the termination of the tenancy, and on the tenant "quitting the holding". It is considered that a tenant that renews its lease cannot carry over the right to compensation into the new tenancy, and should negotiate for a contractual right instead. The position of a tenant that surrenders its tenancy is unclear, and such a tenant should insist on the right being dealt with in the surrender agreement.

Compensation is payable only for improvements made pursuant to the s.3 procedure, and this is where it is useful to have obtained a certificate to that effect, once the works have been completed. Otherwise it will be necessary to prove that the s.3 procedure has been followed and the works done accordingly.

Compensation is available for improvements which at the termination of the tenancy "add to the letting value of the holding". The following improvements do not attract compensation:

- Tenant's and trade fixtures which the tenant is entitled to remove under the general law

- Improvements made pursuant to an obligation for which the tenant received valuable consideration (this may be an obligation owed by the tenant to its landlord or to its own undertenant (*Owen Owen Estate v Livett [1956] Ch 1*)).

It will be appreciated that there are several very common events, such as sub-letting or lease renewal, which might apply to deprive a tenant of compensation.

Also, although contracting-out of the 1927 Act is not possible, there is an avoidance route for landlords which appears to be perfectly legitimate. The landlord cannot be under any liability to pay compensation to the tenant at the end of the lease in respect of improvements which the tenant is under an obligation to reinstate. If the improvements are to be removed, it follows that they will not add to the letting value of the property. A reinstatement requirement will therefore effectively nullify the 1927 Act compensation provisions.

Where a claim is available, time limits apply. These differ according to the way in which the tenancy comes to an end, and they are set out in *s.47, Landlord and Tenant Act 1954*. As mentioned in the preceding chapter, the time limit may be prior to lease expiry: if the lease will expire by effluxion of time, for example, the claim must be made between six and three months prior to the expiry.

The amount of compensation claimed must be specified (*British and Colonial Furniture Co v McIlroy [1952] 1 KB 107*). The maximum amount is the lesser of:

- The net addition to the value of the holding as a result of the improvement, and

- The reasonable cost of carrying out the improvement at the termination of the tenancy.

In relation to the former, a landlord's intention to demolish the property or to make structural alterations to it, or to change the use of the property after the end of the lease term, must be taken into account, and can significantly reduce the amount of compensation.

A claim for compensation under *s.1* is a rarity. One reason for this is that it is only available where a *s.3* notice was served prior to the alterations having been undertaken, and that may often not have been done. However, as suggested earlier, many letters seeking consent for alterations may constitute *s.3* notices, so this requirement may be satisfied more often than is realised.

Also, tenants now have the protection of the *Landlord and Tenant Act 1954*, which was not even on the horizon in 1927. This is relevant for two reasons. First, most tenants have security of tenure, and so tend to stay in the property for longer, so they get full value from any improvements that they make. Secondly the 1954 Act contains its own provisions that require the landlord to pay compensation to the tenant if the landlord refuses to renew a lease on any of the 'no-fault' grounds. Compensation under the 1954 Act is calculated on the basis of rateable value, which means that it is a much simpler system to operate than the procedure under the 1927 Act.

The Law Commission has actually recommended that the compensation provisions of the 1927 Act should be abolished, since they are so seldom used. However, although it is unusual for tenants actually to issue a claim, there is a use to the tenant in having the right to claim, since it can be used to bargain down any dilapidations settlement.

Fixtures

The starting-point, when a tenant brings its own items onto the leased property, is that they stay in the ownership of the tenant. They are chattels. But that is not the case when they are attached to the leased property. They may then be regarded in legal terms as having become part of the land itself – for example, the building materials used in constructing a building on the land, or perhaps an extension to an existing building. Where items are attached to an existing structure on the land, they may become 'fixtures'. These latter two possibilities, taken together, are likely to apply to most of the materials, equipment and structures which a tenant installs in the course of carrying out alterations.

In passing, it is worth noting that although the colloquial expression is 'fixtures and fittings', the law does not recognise any additional category of 'fittings'; an item is either a chattel, a fixture or part of the land. The word 'fittings, despite this, is often found in leases, but it is suggested this is best avoided.

A fixture becomes the landlord's property, so it will benefit the landlord after termination of the tenancy, unless reinstatement is required. The exception to that is 'tenant's fixtures' (otherwise known as 'trade fixtures'). A tenant will be entitled (and quite possibly obliged, by virtue of reinstatement requirements) to remove tenant's fixtures at the end of the lease. It follows that they fall outside the regime under *s.3* of the 1927 Act, because they will not add to the letting value of the property; equally no compensation is payable under *s.1*, by virtue of a specific exception for tenant's fixtures.

Chattels are generally easy to identify. They are loose, unattached items. As the old chestnut has it, you lift up the building, and everything that falls out is a chattel. Equally, it is usually not hard to reach a conclusion as to whether an item has become part of the land. What is not always easy to ascertain is what amounts to a fixture, and within that category what amounts to a tenant's fixture, and there is a considerable body of case-law.

The case of *Peel Land and Property (Ports No 3) Ltd v TS Sheerness Steel Ltd [2013] EWHC 1658 (Ch)* has provided a modern opportunity to revisit the applicable principles, and illustrates that even very substantial and 'permanent' items may be regarded as tenant's fixtures.

The case revolved around major plant at the Sheerness Steel Works in Kent. The claimant was the landlord. A former tenant went into administration in January 2012. The landlord commenced proceedings against the former tenant, seeking an order restraining it from selling, disposing of, interfering with or otherwise dealing with plant and machinery during the term of the lease (which was for 125 years from 1971). The defendant company was established to acquire the former tenant's business and assets, and took an assignment of the lease in June 2012, following which it was substituted as defendant.

The High Court applied the established legal tests to distinguish chattels from fixtures, and to determine which fixtures were removable tenant's fixtures and which accrued to the benefit of the landlord.

Identifying fixtures

There is a twofold test to identify a fixture: the 'degree of annexation' (i.e. attachment to the premises), and the 'purpose of annexation'. As regards degree of annexation, a light fitting may be attached with a sufficient degree of permanence to be a fixture; however, the light bulb which is fitted into it will not be a fixture. It is attached, but not with any permanence, and it can be removed easily and without any damage to itself or the premises. The purpose of annexation, though, is now the dominant test: was the item attached to the premises for the better enjoyment of the item, or for the better enjoyment of the premises? One illustration of what is meant by that was given in *Holland v Hodgson (1872) LR 7 CP 328*, and is often quoted in the caselaw:

> *"Thus blocks of stone placed on the top of one another without any mortar or cement for the purpose of forming a dry stone wall would become part of the land, although the same stones, if deposited in a builder's yard and for convenience sake stacked on the top of each other in the form of a wall, would remain chattels."*

Identifying tenant's fixtures

A tenant's or trade fixture must: (a) have been attached for the purposes of the tenant's trade or for mere ornament and convenience; and (b) be physically capable of removal without causing substantial damage to the land and without losing its essential utility as a result of the removal. So a professional firm's brass name-plaque, screwed or cemented to the front of the building, would certainly be a tenant's fixture; but if the firm refurbished the reception area, installing an architect-designed fitted wooden work-station for the receptionists, the likelihood is that it would be too bespoke to be re-used elsewhere, and would not be a tenant's fixture.

Applying those principles in *Peel*, the court had to consider a lengthy list of items. To pick out just a few:

- Items of electrical equipment comprising two 100-tonne transformers and a 50-tonne regulator, were chattels, since they rested on the ground without being attached in any way.

- A crane running on rails was a chattel, since it was not attached in any way, and the rails were tenant's fixtures, as they could be removed relatively easily, and were installed for the purposes of using the crane for the tenant's trade.

- An electric arc furnace weighing 1,195 tonnes was a tenant's fixture: the evidence was that furnaces such as this could be and were removed and re-used.

- A casting machine, 36 feet high, and weighing approximately 500 tonnes, was also a tenant's fixture for the same reason.

- Two weighbridges comprising a steel platform sitting on load cells on the weighbridge pit, and attached only by a cable, were agreed between the parties to be tenant's fixtures, although the judge considered they might be chattels.

- Another furnace, some 109m long, 20m wide and 8m high, was not a tenant's fixture. It was mainly brick-built on a steel frame, and would be largely destroyed by being removed. This was the only item held by the court to be a landlord's fixture, and it might be queried whether in fact it had become part of the land.

The case illustrates that landlords often underestimate the extent of those parts of premises demised by a business lease which are removable. For that reason, it is not usually a good idea to include a blanket exception of tenant's fixtures from the definition of the demised premises. Specific consideration is required.

It can be appreciated that no hard and fast answer can be confidently given as to whether a particular type of item is a tenant's fixture. A tenant's trunking and wiring, for example, may or may not be fixed with a sufficient degree of permanence to make it a fixture at all. If it is a fixture, it is possible that since it will have been designed and installed for specific applications within a specific structure, it will have little or no utility if removed, and cannot therefore be regarded as a tenant's fixture. But it will be a highly fact-dependent judgement. Pallet racking in a warehouse is likely to be affixed sufficiently to be a fixture, but is it installed for the better enjoyment of the warehouse, or the better enjoyment of the racking itself? Again, ease of removability, and potential for re-use elsewhere, may vary from case to case. The courts have recognised that not all of the caselaw in this area is reconcileable.

The expression 'landlord's fixtures' is sometimes used as a convenient shorthand for 'fixtures other than tenant's fixtures', but can mislead, and has been judicially frowned upon in *Marlborough Knightsbridge Management Ltd v Fivaz [2021] EWCA Civ 989*. In that case the landlord complained that the tenant of a long leasehold flat had breached a term prohibiting the removal of 'landlord's fixtures', by replacing the flat's front door. The court held that the front door was part of the structure, and not to be regarded as a fixture.

Contractual modification

Well-advised landlords and tenants will have thought at the outset about what terms are required for reinstatement, repair and yielding-up, so as to avoid the difficulties which follow from having to decide at lease-end what is or is not a tenant's fixture. The scope for modifying the common law position contractually formed the subject of the appeal in *Peel* (the High Court's classification of the various items was not challenged). In *Peel Land and Property (Ports No. 3) Ltd v TS Sheerness Ltd [2014] EWCA Civ 100*, the issue was the effect of certain terms in the lease.

The key provision was a covenant against alterations:

> *"Not at any time during the said term to erect make or maintain or suffer to be erected made or maintained any building erection alterations or improvements nor to make or suffer to be made any change or addition whatsoever in or to the said premises save in connection with the use of the premises for the purpose of steel making steel rolling and operations ancillary thereto".*

The Court of Appeal agreed with the landlord that 'the said premises' in that clause must be taken to mean 'the said premises *from time to time, including all additions and fixtures*'. Thus, removal of fixtures (even tenant's fixtures) amounted to an alteration, and was not permitted by the clause. The court arrived at this interpretation principally because the lease was a building lease; it included a tenant's obligation to construct the steelworks, so that the entire steelworks constituted an addition, or fixture; if, therefore, (as the tenant argued) 'the said premises' referred only to the premises as originally demised, the clause would not be effective to restrict any alterations whatever to the steelworks, which the court found to be an improbable interpretation.

The decision highlights the fact that while there is a common law right to remove tenant's fixtures, that right can be modified by contract. The potential applicability of a restriction on alterations to the reversal of alterations previously carried out is another lesson to take from the case.

The Court of Appeal's decision left one interesting conundrum: the yield-up covenant in the lease expressly preserved the tenant's right to remove tenant's fixtures at the end of the term. If, however, the effect of the alterations covenant was, as the court held, to prevent the removal of tenant's fixtures during the term, then there would only be the instant of lease expiry at which the tenant could effect the removal. That presents a difficulty even as regards small items, let alone 1,195-tonne arc furnaces. As Rimer LJ recognised:

> "...this would mean that, as the end of the term approaches, the tenant could not start to remove any tenant's fixtures in preparation for his vacation of the premises at the end of the term. That may be so, but I do not regard it as a consideration requiring any different meaning to be attached to [the alterations covenant]".

No doubt the court considered there would be time enough to disentangle that knot when the lease came to an end, in another 82 years' time.

Repair obligations and fixtures

A repairing obligation may extend to fixtures, including tenant's fixtures, or it may not. One view would be that if the tenant is to be required to reinstate alterations, or entitled to remove items, then there is no justification for requiring the tenant to keep those elements of the premises in repair. On the other hand, where reinstatement is at the landlord's option, then it makes sense for the repair obligation to extend to alterations, possibly with the exception of tenant's fixtures.

In the absence of express provision, or circumstances suggesting another meaning (as in *Peel*), an obligation to keep 'the premises' in repair is likely to be interpreted as referring to the premises as originally demised, though everything will depend on interpretation of the particular words used (*Field v Curnick [1926] 2 KB 374*).

It is worth noting, though, that in *Peel* the repair obligation expressly applied to all fixtures, including tenant's fixtures, despite the fact that the lease also provided for the tenant to be able to remove them at the end of the term. In the circumstances of the case, that was plainly necessary: the tenant had been granted a building lease for 125 years, and the landlord wanted to ensure that there would be a functioning steelworks on the site throughout the term. Since the tenant had constructed the steelworks, and since the plant and equipment would certainly require maintenance, upgrading and replacement throughout the term, it was necessary for the repair obligation to extend to fixtures. What is appropriate depends on the context.

It must be the case, however, that where a tenant removes a tenant's fixture at lease expiry, or complies with a requirement to reinstate alterations, any prior failure to repair the items removed can have no effect at all upon the value of the landlord's interest, and hence no damages would be payable. A repair obligation in relation to removable items could therefore only have any practical effect in mid-term, or perhaps if the item were not removed from the premises at lease expiry.

Ownership of items removed in the course of repairs

A novel argument in a novel situation, linking repair obligations with ownership of elements of a property, was raised in *The Creative Foundation v Dreamland Leisure Ltd [2015] EWHC 2556 (Ch)*. In that case, a Banksy mural had been painted on the wall of a building. The tenant removed that part of the wall, and shipped the mural to America for sale. The landlord brought a claim for delivery up of the mural, and succeeded in obtaining summary judgment.

The tenant argued that it was not only entitled but obliged to remove the mural by way of compliance with its repairing obligation, and in the same way as it might be entitled to dispose of, say, a rotten window-frame in the course of carrying out repairs, a term should be implied into the lease to the effect that it became the tenant's property once removed from the building.

The first argument as to the repairing obligation was rejected as a matter of construction, and it was further held that even had that argument succeeded, the second argument could not possibly succeed either. The default position was that every part of the property belonged to the landlord. While it might be possible to imply a term to the effect that the tenant was entitled to dispose of goods removed in the course of repair, that was not the same as a term to the effect that the tenant acquired ownership of them, and in any event, a term which might be appropriate in the case of waste goods would not be appropriate in the case of items with a substantial value.

Reinstatement obligations

Landlords typically require tenants to reinstate alterations at the end of a lease because it is believed that it is easier to re-let empty space. Incoming tenants, it is thought, will be more attracted by flexibility than by the benefit of a former tenant's fit-out. This may depend on the circumstances, of course.

But there are two other reasons for requiring reinstatement as well. First, as already mentioned, requiring reinstatement circumvents the compensation provisions in *s.1, Landlord and Tenant Act 1927*.

Secondly, there is the potential to include reinstatement in a terminal dilapidations claim. In negotiating a payment for dilapidations from outgoing tenants, reinstatement requirements can help to inflate the claim. The basis for calculation of damages for breach of a reinstatement requirement has been covered in the preceding chapter.

The inclusion of a reinstatement obligation may be imposed as a condition of the landlord consenting to alterations. If the tenant resists, a landlord will not be able to impose such a condition unless it is reasonable to do so, because of *s.19(2), Landlord and Tenant Act 1927*. Some leases will contain a blanket reinstatement obligation in any event.

It is increasingly the norm that such a provision will give the landlord flexibility either to require reinstatement or not. The practical issue is when such a requirement has to be notified to the tenant. While some leases will stipulate a time-limit such as two months prior to lease expiry, many are silent on the subject.

The general view in such cases is that notice must be given by lease expiry at the latest (although it must always be a matter of construction of the particular wording used). That gives rise to an obvious difficulty where the landlord gives notice before lease expiry, but too late for the tenant to be able to carry out the reinstatement. The problem for tenants is particularly acute where exercise of a break option is conditional upon performance of tenant's covenants, and the landlord raises a last-minute requirement to reinstate alterations.

There is surprisingly little in the way of help from decided cases. On one view, the parties must have intended that any notice should be given in enough time for the tenant to have finished the work before the end of the lease, and so a time limit may be implied. Against that, the market may be volatile, and it may be hard or impossible to predict the requirements of any incoming occupier until shortly before lease expiry, so it is not obvious that an implied time limit would reflect the intentions of the parties. Also, of course, the parties could easily have incorporated a time limit expressly, which is a significant factor against implying one.

In the absence of an express or implied time limit, a 'too-late' notice would still be valid, so that either (a) the tenant is in breach and liable to pay damages regardless, or (b) the tenant is entitled to remain in the premises after lease expiry to do the work. Neither of those possibilities is unproblematic.

So far the approach taken by the courts has indicated that the landlord is likely to be able to give notice at any time up to lease expiry, and that if there is insufficient time to complete the work, then so long as the tenant has done what it can to put the work in hand by the end of the lease, it is likely to be granted a reasonable time to remain in occupation to finish it (*Plummer v Ramsay (1934) 78 SJ 175*; *Scottish Mutual Assurance v British Telecom plc (18 March 1994, unreported, Official Referees' Court)*; *Matthey v Curling [1922] 2 AC 180*; *Baroque Investments v Heis [2012] EWHC 2886 (Ch)*).

However, none of those authorities is very clear or satisfactory on the point, and the approach raises a number of questions about the terms of the continued occupation. Will the tenant occupy pursuant to some form of licence, or tenancy at will? Should the tenant be required to pay for the continued occupation, perhaps on the basis of compensation for use and occupation?

Carpets, partitions and ceiling tiles

It is striking how often dilapidations disputes arise over carpets, partitions and ceiling tiles: items which in a technical legal sense may be chattels, tenant's fixtures or landlord's fixtures, but which are not in a colloquial sense part of the fabric of the building itself.

Reference was made in Chapter 5 to the case of *Riverside Park Limited v NHS Property Services Limited [2016] EWHC 1313 (Ch)*, which concerned exercise of a break option, and in which internal demountable partitions were held to have been chattels, because they were simply screwed to the raised floor and suspended ceiling (in other words, they failed to pass the 'degree of annexation' test). By contrast, in a New Zealand case, *Short v Kirkpatrick [1982] 2 NZLR 358*, partitions were fixed in a more substantial way to the concrete floor, and were held to be tenant's fixtures.

A particular feature of items such as this is how they may interact. In *Shortlands Investments Ltd v Cargill plc [1995] 1 EGLR 51*, one of the issues concerned ceiling tiles, many of which were in disrepair. The tenant resisted liability on the basis that there was no diminution in the value of the reversion as a consequence of the disrepair to the suspended ceiling. The tiles were rectangular, and no longer manufactured; the industry norm had become square tiles of a standard size in the years since the premises had been let and fitted out. The tenant argued that any incoming tenant would fit out to a modern standard, and would replace the entire ceiling grid, if nothing else in order to accommodate modern light fittings, which could not fit within the existing grid. The tenant further argued that an incoming tenant would remove the partitions, and this would damage ceilings and carpets so that those items would have to be replaced anyway. On the facts, the judge held that at lease expiry it was not foreseeable that an incoming tenant would act in either of those ways, so the tenant did not succeed, but the point illustrates the potential for these factors to interact.

An issue in relation to carpets arose in *South Essex Partnership University NHS Foundation Trust v Laindon Holdings Ltd [2016] EWCA Civ 377*. The premises were originally let pursuant to an agreement for lease, which provided for a substantial programme of tenant's fitting-out works, consisting mainly of the installation of a lift and internal partition works, by contractors engaged by the landlord, but at the tenant's expense. Those works included the lifting, cleaning and re-installation, as far as possible, of an existing system of tiled carpeting throughout the building: the upper floors to be carpeted by re-use of the existing tiles, and the ground floor by a mixture of re-use and replacement to the extent necessary.

Shortly before the end of the term of the lease, the tenant informed the landlord that it would be replacing the tiled carpeting system with broadloom carpet of the same colour and specification (i.e. carpet in strips rather than tiles). In the absence of any complaint by the landlord, the tenant then did so.

It is curious that the landlord failed to object, since broadloom carpeting presents difficult issues for the longer term. Where carpet tiles are used, any tiles which become discoloured, worn or dirty can be replaced (as had happened under the agreement for lease in this case). Where there will be changes in the configuration of partitioning, a tiled system can accommodate them. Neither is true as regards a broadloom system.

Following the termination of the lease, the landlord realised that it had a problem, and claimed that the re-carpeting had not amounted to compliance with the relevant repairing covenant, which provided that the tenant was:

> "...to repair or replace from time to time the Landlord's fixtures and fittings in the Premises as may be or become necessary at any time during or at the expiration of the Term."

The tenant's case was, in the alternative, that:

- the tiled carpets were tenant's fixtures, because the tenant had paid for the re-installation of the tiled carpet system in the premises as part of the tenant's fitting-out works, or

- if the tiled carpets were landlord's fixtures, their replacement by a broadloom carpeting system was a permitted alteration under the alterations clause which provided that:

> "The Tenant may make any internal non-structural alterations to the Building without the consent of the Landlord".

The landlord argued that the alterations clause did not apply because the tiles were landlord's chattels, and therefore not part of 'the Building' for the purpose of the covenant. According to the landlord, the tiled carpets were on any view the landlord's property, but as chattels they fell under 'fittings' in the repairing covenant, and the tenant should therefore have replaced them like-for-like, with other tiles. (This was a rare attempt to argue that 'fittings' had a separate legal meaning from 'fixtures').

It was held that the tiled carpets were landlord's fixtures, regardless of the fact that they were re-laid at the tenant's cost at the start of the term. Much the largest part of the tenant's fitting-out works consisted of the installation of a lift which, on any view, was to become part of the fabric of the building, rather than a fixture, so the fact that the tenant had paid for the fitting-out works was of no weight in deciding to whom the carpets belonged. No-one suggested that, following fitting-out, the carpeting system should in some way be apportioned between the parties for the purposes of identifying whether any particular tile was a landlord's or a tenant's fixture.

As the tiles had been glued to the floors, the court would, if necessary, have regarded them as fixtures. However, the court agreed with the tenant: the unqualified right to make alterations extended to the carpets, whether they were landlord's fixtures or landlord's chattels. It would be a commercial nonsense to construe the clause as permitting alteration or replacement of landlord's fixtures, but not permitting alteration or replacement of landlord's chattels provided within the building for the use of the tenant.

There was, in fact, a right for the landlord to require reasonable reinstatement of alterations, but it had failed to exercise it.

Bargaining chips

These cases emphasise the need to anticipate such issues when consent is given to alterations, and to specify whether repair obligations apply to the alterations, whether the landlord should be able to require reinstatement at lease expiry, and whether the tenant should be entitled to remove items at that time. Some leases will contain, for instance, a specific obligation requiring the tenant to re-carpet in the last six months of the term, which removes all uncertainty about that item, at least.

When these issues have not been thought through, one encounters negotiations at lease expiry in which one party has particularly useful bargaining counters, possibly fortuitously. Where a tenant laid carpet tiles, glued to the floor, which thus became landlord's fixtures, an obligation to leave the carpet in good repair is often one which can be expensive to perform. If carpet was simply laid without being attached in any way and remained a chattel, then the tenant's right to remove it potentially presents the landlord with the considerable expense of re-carpeting before it can re-let. Where carpet was laid up to partitions, and the tenant has the right to remove the partitions, the result will be a carpet left with 'missing' strips where the partitions used to be, and again that represents expense for the landlord.

It is suggested that whenever a tenant carries out work to premises, the parties should document agreement, in relation to each element of the work, on the following four questions:

a) Will the tenant's repairing obligation apply to it?

b) Will its value be reflected upon any rent review or lease renewal?

c) Will the tenant be entitled to remove it at lease expiry?

d) Will the landlord be entitled to require its removal at lease expiry?

It would even be possible to document agreement in tabular form. This might be a tedious exercise, and potentially costly, but the benefits at lease-end should outweigh that.

Summary

Tenants may be able at lease expiry to claim against their landlord for compensation in respect of improvements carried out during the term. For this right to apply, there are procedural requirements which must have been followed at the time of requesting consent for the alterations, and time limits to be observed in making a claim. There are several common events which may deprive the tenant of the right to compensation – accordingly claims are rare. The entitlement, where it exists, has a negotiating value in the context of a dilapidations claim, however.

It will be necessary upon expiry to determine whether items forming part of the tenant's alterations have become part of the land, landlord's fixtures, tenant's fixtures, or have remained as tenant's chattels. This will determine whether the tenant has a right to remove items, and it may also determine whether repair obligations apply to the alterations.

Whether or not the tenant is entitled to remove items, the landlord may be able to require removal pursuant to a reinstatement obligation.

Items such as carpets, partitions and ceiling tiles have the potential to cause particular difficulties in relation to all of these issues.

It is important to consider the lease-end consequences when granting consent to alterations, as these common-law rules are all capable of being modified by contract. When preparing for a dilapidations dispute, it is prudent to consider whether provisions of any licence to alter may conflict with provisions of the lease in relation to reinstatement and repair.

CHAPTER NINE
FAQs

Content

This chapter addresses some questions which commonly arise in relation to dilapidations claims:

- What is the relevance of the next letting or sale?

- What is the position of a sub-tenant?

- What if the breach of repairing obligation has been caused by the landlord?

- What is the impact of MEES?

What is the relevance of the next letting or sale?

It should be apparent from the discussion in Chapter 7 of the effect of *s.18(1), Landlord and Tenant Act 1927* that the likely future of the property at lease expiry is highly relevant to ascertaining the diminution in the value of the reversion. Once the landlord has actually dealt with the property, by re-letting, sale, refurbishment or redevelopment, it might be thought that what has actually happened is the best possible guide to the loss the landlord has actually suffered. Two problems stand in the way of this.

Res inter alios acta

In *Haviland v Long [1952] 2 QB 80*, shortly before lease expiry the landlord concluded terms with an incoming tenant. The new tenant was to carry out the outstanding repairs to the property, while the landlord would reimburse him the cost of the repairs so far as covered by the amount of any damages recovered from the outgoing tenant in relation to the disrepair. The outgoing tenant argued that the consequence of that deal was that there had been no damage to the reversion, and hence no damages were payable. The court, however, held that the agreement with the incoming tenant was *res inter alios acta*, and therefore incapable of affecting rights and remedies as between the landlord and the outgoing tenant.

An arrangement entered into with a third party cannot, therefore, either provide a defence, or reduce the amount of damages. This cuts both ways: it cannot increase the amount of damages either. A landlord may enter into a new letting on terms including a substantial rent-free period in respect of the disrepair, in the expectation of recovering from the former tenant, by way of damages for dilapidations, the amount of the rent which has been forgone. But the lost rent does not conclusively fix the amount of the damages; the tenant may argue that market forces have led the landlord to agree a rent-free period longer than would have been justified by the disrepair, as an inducement to enter into the lease.

Post-valuation date events

The *res inter alios acta* rule is one issue; the other is that the valuation date for *s.18(1)* purposes is the lease expiry date. In theory that means that events after that date are irrelevant for this assessment, although in practice that is far from being the full story.

One exception to that general principle is where the landlord will be bearing the cost of work carried out by the new tenant, either by actual reimbursement or by granting a rent-free period. This may be treated the same as if the landlord were carrying out the work, and the cost of the work may therefore be taken *prima facie* as representing the diminution in the value of the reversion (*Jones v Herxheimer [1950] 2 KB 106*).

More widely, in *Smiley v Towshend [1950] 2 KB 311*, and in *Family Management v Gray [1980] 1 EGLR 46*, the courts have accepted that a post-valuation date event may throw light upon the value of the reversion at lease expiry, because it may corroborate evidence as to how the market may have regarded the premises. It is necessary, however, that there should be some evidence to corroborate. In other words, the event or transaction should bear upon some factor which was regarded as actual or potential at the lease expiry date. A deal or event which the market could not have foreseen, such as a sudden and significant shift in planning policy, would not be relevant.

Thus, in *Family Management v Gray [1980] 1 EGLR 46*, the presence at the property of sub-tenants holding over under the 1954 Act, with full repairing obligations and every intention to renew, led the court to conclude that there was no diminution in value of the reversion as a result of the disrepair. The sub-tenants had in fact renewed their leases, after lease expiry but prior to the hearing of the dilapidations claim, but the relevance of this was as corroboration of the evidence that, at the lease expiry date, that was an eventuality which an incoming purchaser would have regarded as highly likely.

Such transactions may support or undermine the opinions of the valuation experts. For instance, a letting in the weeks or months immediately following lease expiry, on a basis where the landlord has had to grant a rent-free period on account of the disrepair, will throw doubt on the credibility of a tenant's valuer who has confidently stated that the landlord would readily be able to let the property without granting any concessions.

In practice, a court may be very ready to conclude that a transaction sufficiently close to the valuation date, even though taking place after it, is a good indication of what market sentiment was at the valuation date. In *Mather v Barclays Bank Plc [1987] 2 EGLR 254*, the terms actually agreed between the landlord and a third party, after lease expiry, were in effect determinative of the assessment of the 'in disrepair' valuation. In *Firle Investments v Datapoint International [2000] EWHC 105 (TCC)* the judge observed that:

> "...the refurbishment ... which was planned, and in due course implemented, affords cogent evidence of the way in which the only realistic contemplatable hypothetical purchaser would have looked at the realistic commercial possibilities of the building at the term date".

Sale of landlord's interest

It is not just the terms of a new letting which may be relevant, of course, but also those of any sale of the landlord's interest. The *Shortlands v Cargill* type of s.18 valuation is based upon the hypothesis that a buyer would reduce its bid to reflect the cost of repair, and if that is what does in fact happen, then of course that corroborates the landlord's valuation evidence.

All of this means that in concluding terms for a sale, or a new letting, the landlord must have one eye upon the consequences for its dilapidations claim. One issue to be particularly wary of is an assignment of the benefit of the dilapidations claim as part of the deal, whether to a purchaser of the landlord's interest, or to a new tenant. There is no technical legal issue as regards assignment of the cause of action; so long as it was incidental and subsidiary to the grant or transfer of a property interest, it will be valid (*Ellis v Torrington [1920] 1 KB 399*). The problem lies in the fact that the assignee will be able to recover only the damages which the assignor would have been able to recover. If the assignor has let at full market rent, with no concessions to reflect the disrepair, or has sold at full market value, then *s.18(1)* may prevent the recovery of any damages at all by the assignee. The courts have shown themselves reluctant to allow the defaulting tenant to escape liability in this way, though, in *Technotrade v Larkstore [2006] 1 WLR 2926*, and *Bizspace v Baird Corporatewear [2007] 1 EGLR 55*. Nevertheless, the landlord should ideally agree an arrangement which does not run the risk of that defence succeeding.

Re-letting to the sitting tenant

It will often be the case that the property is re-let to the sitting tenant. This may be the result of a voluntary negotiation, or it may be done pursuant to *Part II* of the *Landlord and Tenant Act 1954*. Either way it raises particular issues.

To illustrate, consider the following timeline:

1980 – A lease of a newly-constructed office property was granted for a 40-year term, within the 1954 Act, with a full repairing obligation.

1995 – The tenant carried out substantial alterations.

2020 – Upon expiry, the tenant only required a stopgap tenancy for a further two years, while finalising and implementing plans for relocation, and so a two-year renewal lease was granted.

2022 – The tenant vacated, and the landlord made a dilapidations claim.

Standard of repair

In deciding what is the appropriate standard of repair, we have seen in Chapter 1 that it is necessary to consider the age, character and locality of the property, assessed at the date when the lease was granted. The property is now 42 years old, and the second lease was granted only two years ago, when it was 40 years old; it may be expected that age character and locality will differ very little between the two dates. However, if the relevant date were taken to be the date of grant of the first lease, when the property was new, that might make a very significant difference to the required standard of work. The question whether the second lease was intended to be a completely fresh start, or whether it was intended that the standard of repair should be assessed as at the date of the first lease, can only be resolved by interpretation of the second lease, and that is not likely to be straightforward.

Reinstatement of alterations

As regards reinstatement of the alterations carried out in 1995, on the face of it the premises as altered formed the subject-matter of the demise under the second lease, and an obligation arising under that lease to reinstate alterations would normally only apply to alterations carried out during its term. For the landlord to be able to require reinstatement of alterations carried out during both lease terms, at the expiry of the second, would probably require clear, express provision; in the absence of that, it is perhaps unlikely that a usual reinstatement provision would be interpreted in this way. This is particularly so since under the so-called '21-year rule' in *s.34(1)(c)* and *s.34(2)* of the 1954 Act, the 1995 alterations would have been rentalised upon renewal.

That conclusion might be modified in the light of the decision in *New Zealand Government Property Corpn v HM & S Ltd [1982] QB 1145*. In 1952 the tenant purchased the leasehold of a theatre. In addition the tenant also purchased certain fixtures and fittings such as seats, curtains and carpets which had been installed by the previous tenant. The lease expired at the end of September 1970 and the tenancy continued by virtue of the 1954 Act.

A new lease was executed on 8 February 1973. When the rent came to be reviewed in 1978, the question arose whether all or none of the fixtures or only those annexed prior to the renewal were to be taken into account in fixing the open market rental value. The landlord contended that when the original lease expired and the new lease was entered into, the tenant lost the right it previously had during the term of the original lease to remove the tenant's fixtures and therefore those fixtures were to be taken into account in determining the new rent.

The Court of Appeal held that when the term of a lease expired by effluxion of time or by surrender and the tenant remained in possession by virtue of a new tenancy which followed immediately, or by holding over, or as a statutory tenant under the Rent Acts or on renewal of a lease of business premises, the tenant did not lose its right to remove tenant's fixtures so long as it remained in possession.

Accordingly the rent was to be assessed on the basis that the tenant's fixtures could have been removed by the tenant during the extended time of possession, if it so wished, and they were not to be regarded as part of the 'demised premises' for the purpose of fixing the rent.

That decision was not concerned with reinstatement obligations; how its implications might fit with the reinstatement covenant in the second lease, in relation to any first-lease tenant's fixtures, would again depend on the specific terms. As regards non-tenant's fixtures carried out under the prior lease, the decision could have no application.

Reliance upon prior lease

The limitation period under the first lease has not yet expired, and unless the second lease is capable of being interpreted so as to release the tenant from existing liabilities, it would be possible for the landlord to base its claims upon breach of the tenant's obligations in the former. This does, though, look very similar to *Family Management v Gray [1980] 1 EGLR 46*: the letting, on full repairing terms, at a full rent, may be taken as supporting a view that that was a likely eventuality following expiry of the first lease, and that no diminution in value of the reversion can be proved.

Drafting solution

As already stated, the landlord needs to have in mind the consequences for its dilapidations claim when negotiating terms for any new letting, and this applies even more so where it is the sitting tenant which will be taking the new lease. The additional issues just discussed should be identified and provided for. In the same way, the tenant should be alive to whether it is worth seeking to include a contractual equivalent to the right to compensation for improvements (see Chapter 8).

What is the position of a sub-tenant?

In addition to independent repairing obligations set out in the sub-lease, a sub-tenant will often also covenant to perform the repairing obligations in the head-lease. This may be important where the head-lease is for a long term, but the sub-lease is for a short one; the meaning of 'repair' in the head-lease, and the required standard of repair, may be significantly more onerous than in the sub-lease. If in addition the covenant is construed as including an obligation to indemnify the head-tenant against the consequences of breach, then the sub-tenant will also be obliged to pay the head-tenant's reasonable costs of defending dilapidations proceedings brought by the superior landlord (*Hornby v Cardwell (1881) 8 QBD 329*).

This distinction, between the effect of covenants in the head-lease and that of those in the sub-lease, is illustrated by decisions such as *Walker v Hatton (1842) 10 M&W 249* and *Clare v Dobson [1911] 1 KB 35*, in which the repairing obligations in the sub-lease, although expressed in identical words to that in the head-lease, have been held to be of different effect, given that the leases were granted at different dates and for different terms.

In the absence of any direct contractual relationship, it is not possible for a superior landlord to bring claims directly against a sub-tenant; however, many leases require that, as a condition of permission to sub-let, the tenant must procure that the sub-tenant enters into a direct covenant with the superior landlord to observe and perform the head-tenant's covenants in the head-lease, at least so far as they relate to the sub-let premises. The direct covenant is usually given in the licence to sub-let, or in the sub-lease itself, and a direct claim by the superior landlord against the sub-tenant, on the basis of the head-lease covenants, is then possible.

The superior landlord may of course choose to claim against the head-tenant, on the basis that it is in a better position to pay. That will leave the head-tenant to attempt to pass the claim down to the sub-tenant. The claim against the sub-tenant would raise the issue of *s.18(1), Landlord and Tenant Act* 1927, and any diminution in value of the landlord's interest, meaning (for the purposes of that claim) the head-tenant's interest, which may only be a nominal reversion of a day or two. That should not usually mean that the damages recoverable from the sub-tenant will be nil or nominal, though, because the head-tenant's accrued dilapidations liability to the superior landlord will be taken into account in valuing the interest.

When the claim by the head-tenant against the sub-tenant is brought on the basis of a covenant to comply with the obligations in the head-lease, and to indemnify the head-tenant against the consequences of any breach, the head-tenant can generally expect to recover the amount of any settlement sum paid to the superior landlord. This might not be the case where the superior landlord's case appears to be a weak one, and the amount of the settlement is therefore regarded as unreasonably high

(*Siemens Building Technology FE v Supershield [2009] 2 All ER Comm 900*).

However, it may not be so straightforward to recover the settlement sum if the head-tenant's claim against the sub-tenant is brought on the basis of the independent repairing obligation contained in the sub-lease, since as mentioned above, the effect of that obligation may differ from that of the head-lease repairing obligation.

What if the breach of repairing obligation has been caused by the landlord?

Where a landlord brings a dilapidations claim at lease expiry, with a view to recovering a cash settlement, it is sometimes the case that the claim includes items of disrepair which, although the tenant has had responsibility to remedy them, have been caused by some default or inaction on the landlord's part. The classic example is the lease of the top floor in an office building: the landlord has responsibility for the repair of the flat roof, but it has leaked over a period of time, and the landlord has done nothing to put it right. As a result, there is damage to the suspended ceiling in the tenant's premises, perhaps also to plaster and painted finishes, and to the electrical installation.

At lease expiry, the practical issue has ceased to be that of whether and if so how the landlord could be persuaded or compelled to repair the roof satisfactorily. It is now an issue of whether the tenant can escape liability for the consequential disrepair within its own premises. That depends on whether the landlord's breach of obligation gives the tenant a defence or a counterclaim; in other words, whether it relieves the tenant of the obligation to repair to the relevant extent. This may seem academic, but could affect liability for costs in any litigation.

There is no clear, modern authority directly upon the point. Dicta in *Granada Theatres v Freehold Investment (Leytonstone) [1959] 1 WLR 570* and *Bradley v Chorley Borough Council (1985) 17 HLR 305* support the view that the tenant has a counterclaim for the amount of its liability to the landlord; on the other hand, *Colebeck v The Girdlers Co (1876) 1*

QBD 234 and *Citron v Cohen (1920) 35 TLR 560* suggest that the tenant is not liable where default or inaction by the landlord has had the effect of increasing the burden of the tenant's repairing covenant.

The balance of authority favours the view that the tenant has a counterclaim, and tenants are best-advised to conduct any litigation accordingly.

What is the impact of MEES?

The implementation of Minimum Energy Efficiency Standards ('MEES') by the *Energy Efficiency (Private Rented Property) (England and Wales) Regulations 2015* ('the Regulations') raised new issues, or at least a new context for familiar issues, in relation to dilapidations claims.

The Regulations restrict new or continued lettings of a commercial property after prescribed dates (1 April 2018 for new lettings, and 1 April 2023 for the continuance of existing leases), where the relevant property has an Energy Performance Certificate ('EPC') rating of F or G. To be clear about what that means, the landlord is prohibited from letting after the relevant dates, not directly required to carry out works to achieve a higher EPC rating.

As regards dilapidations claims, it is unlikely that the state or condition of the premises which results in the low EPC rating will itself amount to a breach of the tenant's repairing obligation. Energy-inefficient air-conditioning or heating plant, poor or absent heat insulation, or the presence of single-glazed window units, may all contribute to the low rating, despite those elements of the building being in repair. Since the Regulations do not impose any direct obligation to carry out improvement works, there will be no breach of the tenant's covenant to comply with statutory requirements, either.

That said, if the windows or the heating plant were to be in disrepair, then the appropriate remedial works might well include an element of improvement. Single-glazed windows will have to be replaced by double-glazed ones as a consequence of building regulations. The nearest modern equivalent to the old boiler will invariably be more energy-efficient. Whether works which would, coincidentally, improve the EPC rating in this way fall within the tenant's obligations will in each instance be a matter of interpreting the lease in accordance with the established principles discussed in Chapter 1.

The Regulations are most likely to affect the assessment of diminution in value under *s.18(1)*. If a property cannot be relet as a consequence of the Regulations, then the valuation must reflect that. A judgement will be required as to what a prospective buyer would do. Since the Regulations apply to commercial property, the buyer might conclude that a conversion to residential use would be more commercially realistic. The buyer might, of course, reduce its bid to reflect the cost of upgrading works, and if some of the upgrading would also amount to works of repair, then that has an impact upon the s.18 valuation. However, it may be the case that upgrading would supersede repair work altogether.

There may well also be consequences as regards the loss of rent element of any claim. Significant upgrading works for MEES purposes may suggest that any required repairs could be carried out within the same timescale, effectively removing loss of rent from the claim.

Summary

- While in theory the terms of any new letting of the premises after lease expiry, or of any sale of the landlord's interest, are irrelevant to the calculation of the landlord's claim against the former tenant, in practice they may corroborate any evidence as to the value of the premises at lease expiry. This is because they may confirm or undermine what is claimed to have been the market sentiment in relation to the property at that time. The landlord therefore needs to keep the consequences for the dilapidations claim in mind when negotiating any such transaction. This is particularly so in the case of a letting to the sitting tenant, which raises additional issues.

- Sub-tenants will often have given a covenant to the head-tenant to observe the covenants in the head-lease, and to indemnify them against any breach. That will usually mean that their obligations are identical to those of the head-tenant, and any claim by the superior landlord against the head-tenant can simply be passed down to them. In addition, they will often have covenanted directly with the superior landlord to observe and perform the head-lease covenants, in which case the superior landlord may claim directly against them. If, however, the head-tenant is reliant purely on an independent repair obligation contained in the sub-lease, its effect may differ from that of the repair covenant in the head-lease, and full recovery cannot be guaranteed.

- If disrepair within the tenant's premises has been caused by some default or inaction by the landlord, the tenant is likely to have a counterclaim in any dilapidations dispute, to the extent of its liability to the landlord for those items of disrepair. It is unlikely that the default or inaction on the landlord's part gives the tenant a defence against the landlord's claim, however.

- It is anticipated that the implementation of MEES in April 2018 will have a range of effects upon dilapidations claims, principally in relation to the two limbs of *s.18(1)*, but also in relation to loss of rent.

CHAPTER TEN
MANAGING AND
SETTLING DISPUTES

Content

This chapter considers the conduct of disputes, with particular reference to the Dilapidations Protocol, and the role of expert evidence. It concludes with some brief comments on alternative dispute resolution, formal settlement offers, and common pitfalls in concluding settlements.

In court

Dilapidations claims used to be heard by specialist judges known as Official Referees, and were listed as 'Official Referees' Business'. The specialism of the Official Referees was in technical issues to do with building works and defective buildings, and the Technology and Construction Court was later established to give greater focus to that expertise; the Official Referees became judges of that court. The Technology and Construction Court is now subsumed within the Business and Property Courts, which combine a number of specialist jurisdictions. Accordingly, dilapidations claims are now issued in the Business and Property Courts, and listed in the Technology and Construction Court list.

Procedure for Technology and Construction Court claims is governed by *Civil Procedure Rules Part 60*, together with *Practice Direction 60*. Dilapidations claims will automatically be allocated to the multi-track. Reference should also be made to the *Technology and Construction Court guide*.

Scott Schedule

A distinctive part of the established procedure for dilapidations claims is the 'Scott Schedule' (named after a former Official Referee, who devised it). This is essentially an expanded form of the schedule of dilapidations, with additional columns for the tenant's comments and figures, in order to identify the issues (and to do away with excessively lengthy and complex statements of case).

Pre-action protocol

The Property Litigation Association, together with the Royal Institution of Chartered Surveyors ('RICS'), developed a pre-action protocol to govern the conduct of dilapidations claims in 2002. The full title of the document is the *Pre-Action Protocol for Claims for Damages in Relation to the Physical State of Commercial Property at Termination of a Tenancy*, though it is generally referred to as the Dilapidations Protocol. As the long title indicates, it applies to terminal dilapidations claims, and not mid-term ones, and it applies only to commercial property.

The Protocol aims to improve the standard of dialogue between landlords and tenants in dilapidations claims, with a view to encouraging early identification of the issues, and facilitating settlement. In 2012 it was officially adopted by the Civil Procedure Rule Committee, and so parties to dilapidations claims who fail to observe its terms can expect to be exposed to the risk of costs sanctions. This formal adoption of the Protocol seems to have encouraged compliance, which should translate to a greater number of cases settling sooner, and perhaps also to shorter trials for those which do not.

The requirements of the Protocol are, in summary:

- The landlord should send the tenant a schedule of dilapidations in a form annexed to the Protocol, which separates out repair items from reinstatement, decoration, and works required to comply with statute. Ideally it should be sent electronically, to enable the tenant's surveyor to add comments.

- The schedule must be sent within a reasonable time of termination of the tenancy (generally 56 days). It may be sent prior to lease termination, but if so the landlord must confirm the position when the lease comes to an end.

- The schedule must be endorsed by the landlord's surveyor with a statement that in his opinion all the works set out are reasonably required to remedy the scheduled items of disrepair, that the costings are reasonable, and that full account has been taken of the landlord's intentions for the property.

- Within the same timescale, the landlord should also send the tenant a 'quantified demand', which details the amount and breakdown of the landlord's monetary claim. This document will take into account loss of rent, VAT if applicable, and the impact of *s.18(1)* (though no formal diminution valuation is required at this stage).

- The tenant should respond within a reasonable time (generally 56 days), ideally by way of annotation to the landlord's schedule[1]. If the tenant intends to rely upon any supersession issues, they should be identified at this stage. The response must be endorsed by the tenant's surveyor with a statement that in his opinion the response accurately identifies all the work required, that the costings are reasonable, and that full account has been taken of the landlord's intentions for the property[2].

- Disclosure should generally be limited to the supporting items enclosed with the schedule, the quantified demand and the response.

---

[1] Service of the schedule in an electronic format, and its return marked up with the tenant's comments, together effectively perform the function of the Scott Schedule.

[2] In endorsing the schedule and response, the surveyors should be guided by the RICS Guidance Note on Dilapidations.

- The parties are encouraged to meet to narrow the issues and agree the claim if possible, normally before service of the tenant's response, but at any rate within 28 days after.

- The parties are encouraged to consider alternative dispute resolution.

- Prior to issuing proceedings, the landlord must provide a detailed 'quantification of loss', setting out what part of the scheduled works (if any) it has done, and providing evidence of the cost. If there is any part of the work which it has not done or does not intend to do, it should provide a formal diminution valuation.

- If the tenant intends to rely on *s.18(1)*, it must provide a diminution valuation of its own to the landlord within a reasonable time (generally 56 days of receiving the landlord's quantification of loss).

- The parties should then conduct a final 'stocktake' before proceedings are issued, to see if the claim can be resolved or the issues narrowed.

It might appear that the exchange of formal diminution valuations should come earlier in the process, since the quantified demand and the response must address *s.18(1)* issues. The reason why they are exchanged later on is simply to save expense. In the past, dilapidations claims were often negotiated only between building surveyors, to save incurring further professional fees unnecessarily. Solicitors and valuers might only be involved late in the day, if settlement had not proved possible. The preparation of the formal s.18 valuation does involve a significant cost, and it is understandable that parties are inclined to defer that step, until it is clear that it will be needed. The first version of the Protocol required production of diminution valuations at the outset, as is logical, but this met with a considerable degree of resistance. As the Protocol has evolved, so the exchange of s.18 valuations has slipped back in the order of events.

However, the claim cannot sensibly be conducted or defended without input from a valuer on the likely impact of *s. 18(1)*, albeit on an informal basis. Without that, there can be no cost/benefit analysis to decide whether the claim is worth running at all; nor is it possible to decide the level at which to pitch a *Part 36* offer, or whether to accept one received from the other side.

Like all pre-action protocols, the Dilapidations Protocol is not rigid or mandatory. It sets out the process which the courts would normally expect the parties to follow, but a process which differed in some respects might also be perfectly reasonable. Costs sanctions for non-compliance are not automatic. Parties should be familiar with it, however, and should aim not to depart from it unless there is good reason.

<u>Disclosure and Expert evidence</u>

It is noteworthy that the Protocol states that disclosure of documents can generally be dispensed with in dilapidations claims, so long as the appropriate supporting documentation accompanies the schedule, quantified demand, response, and quantification of loss. In certain cases, there might be factual issues in relation to, for example, the genuineness of the landlord's stated intentions for the property, in which case disclosure will be required.

In the Business and Property Courts, a disclosure pilot scheme which began in 2019 has been made permanent from 1 October 2022, having been broadly welcomed. It aims to make disclosure more proportionate and less unwieldy, one of the key changes being the requirement to give disclosure of key documents at the initial stage of litigation, thus front-loading the work (and the cost).

Factual issues apart, the vast majority of the relevant evidence will consist of expert opinion. It will include evidence from some or all of the following:

- Building surveyors, dealing with the condition of the building, and what work is required or appropriate

- Valuers, addressing the impact of *s.18(1)*

- Mechanical and electrical engineering consultants, covering the state of plant and equipment within the property

- Quantity surveyors, dealing with the likely cost of the required work

- Project managers, assessing the period of time it will take to carry out the work

- Planning consultants, giving their views on the chances of obtaining planning consent for any scheme of works which the landlord has in mind for the property

Not every case will raise issues which require the input of all these experts, and not every case will justify the expense involved in obtaining it. Bearing in mind the courts' overriding objective to deal with cases at proportionate cost, it may be that the judge will require issues concerning plant and equipment, cost of work, and length of time required to get the work done, to be addressed by building surveyors, and will not permit evidence from additional experts in those disciplines. However, it will usually be difficult if not impossible to determine a dilapidations claim without expert evidence from, at least, building surveyors and valuation surveyors.

A potential issue here is the court's power to direct that where there are issues requiring expert evidence, it should be given by one joint expert, rather than by experts on each side. *Practice Direction 35* indicates that *"where possible, matters requiring expert evidence should be dealt with by only one expert"*.

This is likely to be unpopular with clients, whether landlord or tenant. The Protocol effectively requires them to engage experts, at significant expense, before issuing proceedings, so it is galling for the court then to insist upon instruction of a single joint expert, who will need to get acquainted with the facts and arguments completely afresh. Realistically, the clients will not dispense with the services of the experts already retained, since they can assist in evaluating the work of the joint expert. Each client will therefore be paying for one-and-a-half experts, instead of just one. Also, while experts should not act as advocates, clients do feel reassured to have 'their' expert going in to bat for them.

There are no figures to show how often courts do insist upon the instruction of single joint experts in dilapidations claims, but anecdotally it does not happen very often, so it may be that courts are sympathetic to the concerns of the parties.

Alternative Dispute Resolution

Parties are encouraged by the Civil Procedure Rules and the Protocol to consider alternative dispute resolution methods before resorting to litigation. A party that unreasonably refuses to participate in alternative dispute resolution may be subject to adverse costs orders (e.g. *Thakker v Patel [2017] EWCA Civ 117*). Bad reasons for refusing ADR might include:

- complexity of the case

- a bad relationship between the parties

- complex issues of law needing to be determined

- cost of ADR

- belief in having a strong case

Good reasons may be quite limited, for example:

- unreasonable or obsessive conduct by one party

- a genuine test case on an issue of principle, where a court's determination is needed

Moreover, in *Lomax v Lomax [2019] EWCA Civ 1467* (not a dilapidations case) the Court of Appeal held that the court had jurisdiction to order parties to litigation to attend an early neutral evaluation, even if one or both objects.

Mediation (a negotiation facilitated by an independent third party) has a reasonably high success rate, and even in those cases which do not settle in the mediation process, it often acts as a catalyst for the parties to narrow the issues, learning more about the opponent's case, or leading to further successful settlement negotiations. One survey indicated that 36% of dilapidations cases settled within two months of a formal mediation or settlement meeting

Other than mediation, both arbitration and expert determination have their place in dilapidations disputes, and in particular the RICS Dilapidations Dispute Resolution Service offers determination by an independent expert who will not only be trained in deciding disputes but will also be an expert in the field of dilapidations.

Offers and settlements

An even more effective prompt for settlement is a formal settlement offer, whether made under *Part 36*, a Calderbank offer, or a simple without prejudice offer. *Part 36* and Calderbank offers, of course, have more persuasive force if correctly pitched, since they put the offeree at risk as to costs. The same survey as just referred to in relation to mediations showed that 76% of dilapidations claims settled within one month of a formal offer being made.

If a settlement can be reached, there are some common pitfalls to be avoided:

- The landlord's claim will often include VAT; like any other head of damages, there must be actual loss for this to be recoverable, so the landlord's VAT status should be investigated. If it can recover the input VAT on the works, then this should not be paid for by the tenant. Equally, VAT should not be included in the claim if the landlord has no intention of carrying out the works.

- It is important to ensure that the settlement covers all liabilities which are intended to be included. A tenant who thinks the dilapidations settlement represents a 'clean break' in relation to the property can sometimes be caught out when the landlord subsequently raises other matters which were not included in the dilapidations claim, for example, cost of compliance with fire officer's requirements or insurers' requirements.

- It may also be necessary to ensure that the liabilities of all relevant parties have been tied up. A sub-tenant might settle a claim brought by its immediate landlord based upon the repair covenants in the sub-lease, only to find that it faces a claim from the superior landlord, having given a covenant direct with that party to comply with the repair covenants in the head-lease. Or it may be that the landlord chooses to bring its claim against a guarantor, or a former tenant; the current tenant should try to ensure that it participates in the settlement, since it potentially faces a claim by the guarantor or former tenant based upon implied indemnity.

Summary

Dilapidations claims are dealt with by the Business and Property Courts, within the specialist Technology and Construction Court list. The Pre-Action Protocol for Dilapidations Claims should be complied with prior to issuing proceedings, unless there is good reason to depart from it, otherwise there is a risk of costs sanctions being applied.

Expert evidence is central in dilapidations claims, and the challenge for the court is to limit the cost as appropriate to the claim. This may lead the court to direct that expert issues be addressed by one joint expert, instead of one for each side.

Alternative dispute resolution and formal settlement offers are both useful tools for prompting settlements. In concluding settlements, common errors include: failing to consider whether VAT on the cost of works can properly be recovered; failing to include all liabilities in the settlement; and failing to include all relevant parties in the settlement.

CHAPTER ELEVEN

THE WIDER PERSPECTIVE

Content

This chapter considers the impact of shorter lease terms and market uncertainty on matters such as rental structures and repairing obligations, questioning the need for including tenant's repairing obligations in leases. It also considers the environmental impact of the 'fit-out and strip-out' cycle, and ways in which changes to conventional practice might be encouraged.

Shorter terms

The pre-existing movement to shorter lease terms in many sectors has been accelerated by the past few years of global uncertainty, as the credit crunch and financial crisis of 2007/2008 was followed by the Brexit vote in 2016, and the ensuing years of associated political turmoil, then the global Covid-19 pandemic beginning in 2020, and most recently the Russian invasion of Ukraine, with the accompanying energy and cost of living crises. Occupiers are understandably shy of entering into lengthy and expensive lease commitments with so much uncertainty remaining, not least over whether familiar patterns of travelling to workplaces will largely resume, or be replaced to a significant extent in the long term by distance working. Flexibility is prized, and investors, too, can see benefits in being able to respond to changing circumstances in a relatively nimble fashion, taking advantage of vacancies to upgrade premises or re-purpose them.

The upshot is shorter leases, and more frequent break options. That in turn means a higher rate of tenant churn, which has implications for conventional lease forms. The familiar rack rent lease, with five-yearly upward-only rent review, a tenant's full repairing liability, and a service charge underwriting any obligation on landlords as regards maintenance and repair, is increasingly unattractive to tenants.

Inclusive rents

Alternative rental structures are in demand, principally rents calculated to some extent at least upon the turnover the tenant generates from the premises. Traditionally, turnover rents have been largely limited to the retail and hospitality sectors, but businesses are increasingly exploring ways of doing something similar in other sectors.

Another rental structure which has also become more popular, and which is not confined to specific sectors, is the inclusive rent. The tenant pays a flat rate, while the landlord bears the risk of fluctuations in the cost of insurance, rates and property maintenance. This is, of course, the antithesis of the 'full repairing and insuring' or 'clear' lease, and many landlords will still not be prepared to grant leases on this basis. However, such ideas are not eccentric or left-field, but are reflected to a greater or lesser extent in, for example, the *RICS' Small Business Retail Lease*, and the *BPF's Short-Term Commercial Lease*.

We have outlined previously how the historic shortening of lease terms has led to the limiting of repair obligations, typically by means of a schedule of condition. The shortcomings of schedules of condition have also been discussed, and it has been suggested that tenants can perhaps think creatively about other ways of limiting the repair obligation, such as a financial cap, or an obligation to spend a certain sum per year on repair, or excluding identified elements of the building (e.g the roof) from the obligation to repair.

It is a short step to questioning why leases must include a tenant's repairing obligation at all. The content of this book up to this point is ample evidence that enforcing repair obligations is by no means a simple, certain or inexpensive matter. Although tenants routinely sign up to full repairing obligations, experience suggests that for the most part they will undertake whatever repairs may become necessary for their own operational requirements or convenience, but will leave everything else to be negotiated at the expiry of the lease. Typically, at lease end, the landlord expects to receive some settlement in relation to dilapidations, and typically that is the outcome.

Getting to that point is likely to have involved paying significant amounts of money to professionals, and probably neither landlord nor tenant will be happy with the amount of the eventual payment. Does the landlord spend that settlement in carrying out the repairs to the building which it has spent months arguing are necessary? It is not obliged to, and very often it will do the bare minimum required in order to achieve a letting. These arrangements, though familiar, are not obviously an efficient way of securing the maintenance of buildings.

Under an inclusive rent structure, the tenant will pay a higher rent in recognition of being relieved of the open-ended repair liability, while the landlord can do as much or as little in the way of repairing the building as it considers sensible. At lease end, there need be no heartache about:

- recovering schedule costs

- complying with the Dilapidations Protocol

- obtaining evidence as to the state of repair, the cost and timing of repair work, or the valuation of the property

- deciding whether certain items constitute repair or improvement

- identifying what items are fixtures and what are tenant's fixtures, and what the impact of that is upon the claim.

Whether such terms are acceptable to landlords will be circumstance-dependent, but inclusive rents have their place, and may become more prevalent.

Environmental impact

With shorter lease terms, and tenants moving on more frequently, there is increasing disquiet about the 'fit-out and strip-out' cycle, from the point of view of the impact on the environment. It is all too common to see a perfectly good fit-out thrown away so the landlord can market a clear property, followed by the incoming tenant installing their own fit-out, not essentially very different from the previous one.

Where landlords are obliged, as they commonly are, to act reasonably in considering requests for consent to tenant's non-structural internal alterations, the environmental impact of the proposed alterations has not yet featured in caselaw as being among the matters which a landlord may reasonably take into account. This could change; 'reasonableness' can encompass many factors which will change as society and the world changes. Landlords could put it beyond doubt by incorporating into the alterations clause specific provision that in considering what is reasonable they may have regard to the effect upon energy efficiency, what materials are to be used, and the anticipated life of the proposed alteration.

Tenants may see a downside in increased restriction upon their freedom to carry out alterations, but there is an upside too, in that the corollary should be limitations upon landlords' ability to require reinstatement. For example, reinstatement may be considered unnecessary and inappropriate where the tenant's alterations have improved the EPC rating. Perhaps certain standard alterations could be identified as not requiring reinstatement; perhaps reinstatement might be made subject to a requirement for landlord's reasonableness, having regard to the environmental performance of the property. It may encourage tenants to put money into alterations which improve the environmental performance of a building if they know that they do not face the cost of reinstatement at lease expiry.

With shorter terms, occupiers in certain sectors, such as offices, increasingly seek demountability. As a halfway house between stripped-out premises and serviced accommodation, landlords will increasingly market premises with a second-hand fit-out, or install fit-out themselves in accordance with a scheme agreed with the tenant. Offices are increasingly open-plan and flexible, and prefabricated meeting rooms or pods may be preferred to so-called demountable partitions, which in practice are rarely relocated.

It seems inevitable that pressure on both investors and occupiers to take into account the environmental impact of alterations and reinstatement will grow, whether from government, professional bodies, or the concerns of staff.

Summary

Shorter leases and greater economic uncertainty have led to more frequent changes of occupier, and pressure on traditional lease terms. Inclusive rents are now more frequently seen, as landlords begin to question the benefits of the traditional tenant's repairing obligation. More frequent 'fit-out and strip-out' also raises environmental concerns, and it seem inevitable that practice in this regard will change.

MORE BOOKS BY
LAW BRIEF PUBLISHING

A selection of our other titles available now:-

'A Practical Guide to Parental Alienation in Private and Public Law Children Cases' by Sam King QC & Frankie Shama
'Contested Heritage – Removing Art from Land and Historic Buildings' by Richard Harwood QC, Catherine Dobson, David Sawtell
'The Limits of Separate Legal Personality: When Those Running a Company Can Be Held Personally Liable for Losses Caused to Third Parties Outside of the Company' by Dr Mike Wilkinson
'A Practical Guide to Transgender Law' by Robin Moira White & Nicola Newbegin
'Artificial Intelligence – The Practical Legal Issues (2nd Edition)' by John Buyers
'A Practical Guide to Residential Freehold Conveyancing' by Lorraine Richardson
'A Practical Guide to Pensions on Divorce for Lawyers' by Bryan Scant
'A Practical Guide to Challenging Sham Marriage Allegations in Immigration Law' by Priya Solanki
'A Practical Guide to Legal Rights in Scotland' by Sarah-Jane Macdonald
'A Practical Guide to New Build Conveyancing' by Paul Sams & Rebecca East
'A Practical Guide to Defending Barristers in Disciplinary Cases' by Marc Beaumont
'A Practical Guide to Inherited Wealth on Divorce' by Hayley Trim
'A Practical Guide to Practice Direction 12J and Domestic Abuse in Private Law Children Proceedings' by Rebecca Cross & Malvika Jaganmohan
'A Practical Guide to Confiscation and Restraint' by Narita Bahra QC, John Carl Townsend, David Winch
'A Practical Guide to the Law of Forests in Scotland' by Philip Buchan
'A Practical Guide to Health and Medical Cases in Immigration Law' by Rebecca Chapman & Miranda Butler
'A Practical Guide to Bad Character Evidence for Criminal Practitioners' by Aparna Rao
'A Practical Guide to Extradition Law post-Brexit' by Myles Grandison et al

These books and more are available to order online direct from the publisher at www.lawbriefpublishing.com, where you can also read free sample chapters. For any queries, contact us on 0844 587 2383 or mail@lawbriefpublishing.com.

Our books are also usually in stock at www.amazon.co.uk with free next day delivery for Prime members, and at good legal bookshops such as Wildy & Sons.

We are regularly launching new books in our series of practical day-to-day practitioners' guides. Visit our website and join our free newsletter to be kept informed and to receive special offers, free chapters, etc.

You can also follow us on Twitter at www.twitter.com/lawbriefpub.